THE 12 VIRTUES OF THE EXTRAORDINARIES

How to Conquer Fear and become the Best Version of Yourself

To my mum, who believed in the reality of my dream, irrespective of my disability, and to my lovely wife Mide, who encouraged me to explore my potential and create the best version of me.

Author: Ayo Jimmy

Title: The 12 Virtues of the Extraordinaries

ISBN-978-1-9997685-3-9

Category: Personal Development/Self Help/Personal Growth/Mental Health/Learning Disability/ Wealth creation/General.

Publisher: MIH Publishing

THE 12 VIRTUES OF THE EXTRAORDINARIES

How to Conquer Fear and become the Best Version of Yourself

Ayo Jimmy

MIH Publishing

THE POWER OF PUBLISHING IS AT YOUR FINGERTIPS

FOREWORD

In life, you have two sets of people, the ones that live by excuses and the ones that live for a purpose. I have had the awesome privilege of working with Ayo Jimmy and have seen him to be a purpose driven being with a tremendous passion to help others become, live and be the best person that they have the ability to be.

Ayo Jimmy in his book: **The 12 Virtues of the Extraordinaries** tackles the many issues of society today that holds back individuals from living to their best and highest potential. In order for one to become the best version of themselves one would have to recognize the stumbling blocks that is barricading them in their room of fear and limitation but more importantly they need to have the right information and knowledge in order to take the action that will get them out of that dark room. Information without action is as equal to action without information. Imagine being in possession of a powerful car; these days it's the Bugatti and Maserati - so let's say it's the Maserati Quattroporte, the engine in this car generates a maximum power output of 336 PS (247 kW; 331 hp) which is indeed powerful, imagine you have it but it has no fuel or another option you have the fuel and the car but no driver – Pointless! In both scenarios despite having this car with this exceptional engine it will be of no use.

Ayo Jimmy in this extraordinary book not only provides the

information but also propels you to implement and take the necessary actions that will enable you to truly live your purpose and highest potential, even greater to become an extraordinaire. Do read and enjoy a beautiful work of art through words as Jimmy takes you on various journeys of conquering your fears and becoming the best version of yourself.

MICHELLE WATSON

Multiple Award Winning Speaker, Book Creation Mentor, Author of Two International Bestseller and CEO of Breakfree Forever Consultancy

CONTENTS

"The hunger for victory is everything, not victory itself. Make losing painful enough that it will ignite your desire to manifest victory."

-Ayo Jimmy

OPENING WORDS

"People of accomplishment rarely sat back and let things happen to them. They went out and happened to things."

-Leonardo Da Vinci

Every human being on this spinning planet has the ability to rewrite their history but it all starts with our desire for change. Life, being what it is, has the tendency to test our desire for confirmation of how badly we really want the change that we aspire for, and fear is the name of the game. We can play life at its game by feeling our fears to fuel our actions and not be filled by it. For sure, there will always be setbacks and adversity will encroach our precious moments but it's only the people who keep their fear in check by transforming it into a weapon to propel their action that become the extraordinaries and live to achieve success beyond their own imagination. The reality is that we will all experience fear and we will continue to experience fear as long as we live on this planet but the solution to overcoming our fear comes from one thing and one thing alone: understanding the relationship between fear and success through consistent action.

Are you achieving what you want in life or are you crippled by your fear? Here is what you must understand: avoidance of life challenges is not safer than exposing oneself to them and the difference between the "shakee" and shaker of the world of greatness is how they use their fear to formulate the blueprint for their fulfillment. This book contains stories of higher

1

achievers who engraved their footprints on the golden map of history because of their ability to use their fear to their advantage. From the interviews with some of the most successful people on the planet and the research works of icons found here you will notice that most of the great achievers mentioned in this book come from different backgrounds, social classes and ethnicities but the commonality in all of them is that they all started from nothing but ended up at the pinnacle of success because they chose to take control of their destiny by acquiring the secrets that defy the power of fear and converting them into virtues that ignite their actions for successful achievement.

The success they have achieved is clearly the result of consistent practice and persistence, not privileges or luck. Their stories also reveal how the virtues, if well mastered, can open us to the reality of our own dreams and empower us with tremendous power to create our destiny by following their footsteps. Each chapter contains iconic stories of the determined who exemplify courage to overcome life's obstacles at all cost. The action plan at the end of each chapter gives you a detailed outline of how to adapt these concrete ideas and this knowledge to your circumstances.

One word of caution, please do not gallop through this book from page one to the last. Take notes, pause from time to time and reflect. If possible have someone to discuss what you read in this book with. The aim of this book is to open your eyes to those secrets and inspire you to master their use to program yourself for greatness. Remember, those who program themselves for success find a way to enhance their success against all odds. The blame game is for those who still wallow in their state of ignorance. Don't let that be you!

I encourage you not just to read this book but to read it with the intention to create change by taking action. Great opportunities lurk at every corner of our life, waiting for the person with the desire for change to come along and discover them. It is my sincere hope that as you read this book you will discover that your fear is your weapon for waging war against the situations and circumstances of life and not what you should allow to imprison your actions from the change that will elevate your greatness.

Hopefully you will find this book helpful on your journey to creating the best version of yourself and if your life should change for the better because of this book I would love to hear from you if our path should cross.

> *"The cost of wisdom is half the price of ignorance. Let adversity keep you humble and challenges make you strong."*
>
> *-Ayo Jimmy*

Visit my website for more information on one-on-one business consultation with me.

WEBSITE: http://passionateachievers.com

CHAPTER 1

DEFINE VISION
CREATE DESTINY

"The only thing worse than being blind is having sight but no vision."

-Helen Keller

We all have 24 hours in a day and seven days in a week on this spinning planet. Have we ever wondered some people are more successful and achieving their desires more than others? Why are some people earning more money and living an abundant life and others remain continuously worried about financial limitations? Knowing and understanding our purpose in life is essential to the fulfillment of our greatness on this planet. Our life purpose stems from our desires, which originate from our vision. We all have a purpose for living and that purpose is the road map that makes our lives masterpieces. While some people are willing to trade the security of a regular paycheck to follow their vision, others are not because the reality of their vision is unclear and encompassed by the unknown. Why is that so? The hard truth about this billion-dollar question is that a lot of people don't really know their reason for living. We can only find this out by being obsessed with solving problems that align with our 'why'.

Our vision is embedded in our why. Vision creates the fundamental necessity to attaining a meaningful and fulfilling life. It reflects on who we are, our authentic self. Vision acts as a flame that lights our path through the turbulent times of life. It gives impetus to our mission and action. Our vision drives our life to a stratosphere of its extraordinary experience and makes room for the unimaginable to be available. *Jonathan Swift once wrote, "Vision is the art of seeing what is invisible to others."*

Defined vision is the force within that propels relentless action and ignites our belief to forfeit the present for the unknown journey of the future. Defined vision invents what is not in existence because of our capability to see beyond our present state of reality. It fuels the power of passion to its highest state of commitment and provides us with the ability to see past our natural sight and present circumstance. "Defined vision creates the vivid concept of imaginative contemplation". The more specific the vision is, the more likely it will be fulfilled. A defined vision helps in the pursuit of our dreams and the achievement of goals. It provides the cornerstone for us to visualize and articulate the possibility of the future that grows and improves. Having a concrete vision helps us to keep our priorities right when it comes to decision making.

Andrew Carnegie, Richard Branson, Martin Luther King Jr, Bill Gates, Michael Jordan, Oprah Winfrey, Sam Walton and Elon Musk-do these names ring a bell? Yes, they do and you may recognize them for something in particular-the achievement of greatness, which results from defined vision. Those without a defined vision spend their lives taking the path of least resistance as they try to avoid discomfort. They live in full paradise of their own comfort zone and allow their true potential to be imprisoned till death. Our day-to-day decisions will get trapped in the tyranny of urgency without a super-specific defined vision. The purpose of having a defined vision for our life is to enable us to live an exciting and fully engaged life. Defined vision helps us to know why we are doing what we are doing and to ignite our desire to sign up for the manifestation of our unlimited greatness. It begets a vivid emotional passion that describes a brief movie of our journey to breakthrough.

Creating a vivid vision requires us to have a why. Our why solidifies our vision and enhances our ability to bring it to life. Too many people avoid creating a vision for their lives, not because the exercise is too futile but because they don't have a reason for crafting one. The harsh reality is that if we don't have a reason for living we will only help others live the reality of their vision, which they believe in. Without a reason for having a vision our hope of accomplishment is critically at stake and at the mercy of hope. The importance of fulfilling our dreams can only be examined through the lens of our why. Identifying your why is one of the most effective strategies to energizing achievement of the abundant life of happiness that you were born to live. The first part to discovering our why for creating a defined vision is to take it from the unseen world and bring it into the natural realm.

The amazing story of the 38th Governor of California, Arnold Schwarzenegger, is a great real-life account that illustrates how identifying his why helped shape his decision to create his vision. Arnold's vision was to become the best bodybuilder of all time. The desire to actualize his life vision started to unfold when he came in contact with a magazine which had Reg Park on the front cover with the title *Hercules and the Captive Women*. He read through the magazine and the blueprint of his why became clear to him. Arnold from then on started to see Reg Park as the role model for achieving his vision. He started to train and lift weights; he would break into the gym and train until he collapsed from total exhaustion. In his documentary filmed by ESPN films, Arnold mentions that apart from putting up pictures of Reg Park, Muhammad Ali and other power lifters all over his bedroom wall to remind him of his vision and enhance his determination to win the body-building championship over and over again, when he worked in the gym he maintained a smile and positive outlook knowing that every rep and extra weight lifted was pushing him one step closer to bringing his vision to reality. His dream was finally realized when he went AWOL from the Austrian army to take part in the body building competition, which was to earn him the title Mr. Europa Junior. Two years later with much muscle pumping, Arnold became the youngest ever Mr Universe.

We all have a defined vision. Identifying why we exist and how to use this reason to create the best version of who we truly are is essential to our breakthrough in life. Here are some of the simple steps that we can follow to discover our why in life.

> *"It is easy to create wealth but it is hard to create a concrete vision."*
>
> -*Ayo Jimmy*

1. **Define what success means to you.**

   Having a clear sense of purpose on what your interpretation of success is will define how hard you are willing to strive and take risks to make it happen. A viable answer to this key question will keep you motivated and enable you to start setting your own terms for the vision achievement. It will also link you to causes that are congruent with the real you in you. Without a distinctive explanation of what success truly means to us, we will fall into a state of disillusion as to why the accomplishment of a vision is essential to our living. To avoid getting entrapped by distraction and a sense of despair we need to critically define what success means to us in its totality.

2. **Identify your passion.**

We all have something within us that makes us step away from societal expectation and focus on what we expect from ourselves. Our calling is the masterpiece that provides us with the zest to jump out of bed with hunger for greatness and life transformation. It is very hard to improve your life if you don't know what you are passionate about. Our passion is the key that connects what matters to us in life and our success.

Everyone is unique and our uniqueness radiates through our passion. Identifying what we are passionate about is not a rhetorical question that will take us a lifetime to figure out. It is that spectacular feeling that connects us with our childhood dreams of how our life should be. The indisputable thing about passion is that it is infectious and when it is uncovered it will intuitively motivate us to make a difference in the world around us.

3. Define what matters to you in life.

When you know what matters to you in life it is easier to bring it into existence. Defining what matters to you in life will enable you to create a vivid picture of what you want your life to look like and how you are willing to sacrifice your present state for your future glory. It will put you in a sweet spot where playing it safe is no longer an issue in your life's master plan.

Envisioning what matters to you in life will provide you with a greater chance of living life to its fullest. It will trigger thoughts and ideas that will naturally lead to the grandest vision for your future. Your true meaning of what matters in life could be an intersection that lies between your talent, skills/expertise, passion and their deepest values. Discovering it and why it matters to you will release an inner potential that will define your passion and persistence to become the best version of yourself.

Record Your Vision on Paper

A recorded vision gives the visionary the momentum and equips them with the power to overcome resistance. It brings out the irresistible gut and grit to take action and live the life that one so desires. The secret to vision accomplishment is to commit it in writing. Dr. Gail Matthew's research on 267 goal setters shows that we have a 42 percent chance of achieving our vision if it is recorded on paper or on any form of electronic device. Recording our goals enables us to reflect on their importance. It will force clarity out of our inner mind and enable us to articulate the importance of our intention. Having various opportunities can become a distraction overnight but maintaining a list of written goals will enable us to evaluate each opportunity and design a master plan for achievement. Taking fifteen to twenty minutes to document your daily vision will turn it into a written list of concrete goals.

Vision held in the mind has the possibility of evaporating, with over 1500 thoughts per minute passing through our minds daily. We are able to visualize our vision when it is written down and displayed on our restroom mirror, by our work desks or kept in our wallets. There will be more clarity to our vision if we look into our hearts and create its prototype on paper or any form of electronic device. The future belongs to those who see the possibilities and capture them on paper before they become obvious. Wherever we want to be in life is ingrained in our vision and our ability to record it in our journal. Don't use your head as the filing cabinet. Here is an intriguing story on how recording vision on paper can easily shape the realization of our destiny.

Andrew Carnegie was a notable Scottish-American self-made steel tycoon and one of the wealthiest businessmen of the 19th century, whose journey to riches started when he recorded his vision on a yellow sheet of paper in his twenties. Mr. Carnegie wrote a note to himself stating that he was going to use the first half of his life to accumulate money and spend the last half of his life giving it all away. He got so inspired by this vision that he accumulated over 450 million dollars; the equivalent of four and a half billion dollars in today's currency. Recording his vision was one of the propelling forces that ignited his inner desire to ensure that he saw the reality of his vision. Napoleon Hill, when he was 16 years old, adopted Andrew Carnegie's philosophy when he wrote his vision to become a millionaire by age 23 on paper. Although he became a laughing stock to his friends, capturing his vision on paper drove his ambition so much that he wrote Think and Grow Rich, a world-changing book that turned his life around and made him one of the richest men on this planet.

When it comes to vision, the extraordinary people do not use their heads as a filing cabinet because the art of creativity lies with the visualization archetype the core manuscript of who we truly are. Life transformation starts with recording our vision on paper. Here are some of the most powerful reasons it is essential to record your vision on paper and modern day devices.

1. **It enhances self-discovery.**

    The true divinity of who you are radiates when you record the innate part of you on paper. Recording your vision in a personal diary opens the channels of communication with self. It creates the joy of discovering who you are, who you want to become and how far you are willing to go in transforming your life to build the real you. <u>Writing your vision down is not only an act of revealing your inner wisdom; it is also a way to secure the architectural design of your future masterpiece</u>. It provides you with an answer to a bigger life question on who you truly are. Record-keeping your vision allows the real you to show up on a blank page before the pessimistic doom of doubt has the chance to take over your subconscious mind. According to Sandy Grason, the author of Journalution, documenting your vision is a profound way of revolutionizing your soul.

It is the inspiration that emerges when doubt and fear are imprinted on a blank page with the true reality of who you want to become in the future. It is putting the philosophical belief regarding your state of mind into an act of commitment and willingness to create the best version of yourself. Committing your vision to paper enables you to consider who you are at different points in time and gives you the liberty to let your future resonate with your present state of mind. It enlightens you about yourself by enabling you to love who you are and be the designer of your life's purpose.

2. **It provides a sense of direction.**

The unique secret for achieving any vision lies in one's ability to record it in a diary. Unwritten visions are mere fantasies. Keeping a written statement of your vision prevents interference and distraction by giving you a concrete end point to aim for and get excited about. It enables you to choose an achievable time frame and measurable details for its accomplishment so you know exactly where you are at every stage.

Vision documentation motivates you to take action as you divide each activity on your life's to-do-list into manageable steps and become accountable for the progress of each of these baby steps. One good reason we write our vision down is to build the road map that will steer us to our destination. Writing your vision down gives you that sense of direction which not only reaffirms your belief in its reality but also instructs your subconscious mind to create an action plan and follow-up strategy for its achievement.

3. It enables you to stay focused.

Writing your vision down and scheduling dates for its evaluation will keep you on track and motivate you to hold your momentum during the hard times. It is imperative you note down your experience while in pursuit of your vision this will inspire you to remain focused. It will provide you with an excellent view of your progress in achieving your desired objectives. Recording your vision is also a visual reminder that will help you to stay focused on working toward the fulfillment of your abundant life by drawing your attention to why you set the goal in the first place.

In effect, to get your subconscious mind on board with your ultimate vision, you need to know what you want to achieve and create your life desire on paper. Writing your vision down on paper provides you with the time management system to enable you build that hyper-focused maintenance strategy and increases the likelihood of successfully achieving the unlimited life of greatness that you aspire to live for a lifetime. The reality is documenting your vision prevents distraction and procrastination. It builds your confidence and strengthens your persistence toward harnessing your breakthrough.

Your Belief is Important to Vision

"Seeing-is-believing is a blind spot in man's vision."

-R. Buckminster Fuller

Unshakeable belief in your vision often attracts open doors to various strategies that will enhance ability to achieve the unimaginable. When belief is attached to vision, the how-to-achieve the vision always takes care of itself. We begin to magnetize the resources for its fulfillment. People around us may not believe in the reality of our vision, which is not unusual to every great achiever. We have to know what the desired outcome feels like and identify what to do in order to make it happen. To harness our vision, it is essential that we surround ourselves with people who believe in the reality of our dreams. Belief is the starting point for every great achievement. It keeps our vision alive and reassures us that we have a free ticket to abundant life.

"As long as you believe in your own vision, you have something but when you give up on your vision, you become personally bankrupt."

-Ayo Jimmy

Having the courage to remain truthful to our belief system while in pursuit of our vision is as important as knowing what action to take to make our dreams come true. In turning our vision to reality, we need to know what action to take and never stop pushing and believing in the possibility of its achievement. Creating this grandest vision will require hard work, determination and dedication. Taking a massive leap toward success and clothing our minds with belief will enable

15

us to live the abundant we have always aspired for. The winning formula for great success is to have faith in our vision and to take one step at a time. According to Blake Roney, *"Believing in your potential and vision is paramount to success."* Let's take a quick glance through the diaries of some extraordinary people and see how believing in their vision has helped shape their destinies.

Thousands of distributors that join Nu Skin, the anti-aging personal care and nutritional supplement product, every year have no idea the amount of courage and tenacity it took for the company co-founder Blake Roney to create and persevere in building this successful business venture. At one point a marketing expert who happened to be his college professor dismissed his business idea and told him it wouldn't work. Blake and his co-founder refused to listen to the negative comments they encountered and decided to have an unusual belief in their instinct and vision. Each day the founders put innovation into their evolving growth, not only in the way they formulated their products, but also in how they paid their distributors. Today, the firm can claim operations in 52 countries around the globe through a network of approximately 1.2 million independent distributors and counts itself as one of the largest direct selling companies in the world. The company's global operations have generated more than $2.25 billion in revenue.

There's also a famous story about William Henry Gates III, popularly known as Bill Gates, a worldwide giver of epic proportions who changed the world through his belief in the personal computer as a game changer for human existence. He built the world's largest software business that changed the world completely; about 90 % of the computers we use today use Windows Operating System, which is made by Microsoft, a company founded by Bill Gates. Imagine the impact he has on the world as a result of believing in his vision. It's our vision for a reason. We might not be able to change our past but we can transform our future if we believe in the reality of our vision. To put the concept in its simplest form, this is why it is critical to believe in your vision.

1. **It makes your life worth living.**

   Finding the true meaning for living requires your ability to believe in the reality of your vision. Without truly identifying who you really are and why you exist to pursue a meaningful life, you are denying yourself the ability to find your unlimited potential and value in life. Believing in your vision creates that inborn vigor to push the limits to their max and strive to turn your lifetime dreams into reality. According to Albert Camus, *"Our life is worth what we want it to be worth."* A life without vision is depressing but a life with vision has an interpretative meaning for living a worthy life. Your vision should be the major thing that gets you up passionately every morning. Your hearty belief in its reality will inspire you to bring out the best in yourself and face the challenges of life when they rear their ugly heads.

   When we believe in our vision, our enthusiasm for its achievement and the confidence to make it happen increase beyond measure. We become determined to figure out what the next step will be and our courage is energized to labour toward its fulfillment. Experiencing unique and invaluable living is associated with our belief in what we exist to contribute to the planet. Believing in our vision gives our life a profound meaning that makes us worthy of living.

2. **You will be an inspiration to others.**

One thing that makes us iconic in our own space is the belief that we attach to our vision. Apart from becoming believers who preach the gospel of inspiration of our newfound love to others, believing in our vision allows our confidence to overshadow our fear because it tables the reality of who we want to become before our imagination. We are not only motivated by its possibility, we also have that innate courage to continuously tell the stories in our own unique ways to motivate others to make a move in life to become someone and never give up. It is this connective mechanism that links us with people who also believe in the reality of their true potential, the dream chasers of life.

Believing in our vision put us in that state of freedom where we are not afraid to speak out and share our vision joyfully with whomever cares to listen. Believing in our vision and happily sharing its realization with the world will put us at the mercy of those who are willing to help with its fulfillment. Dr. Martin Luther King Jr.'s speech shared an intriguing vision that continues to impact American history because of the belief he had in it.

3. It will shape our future

Our belief honours our creativity and propels us to live its reality. The belief that we hold toward our vision helps to shape and design our life. Successful people don't achieve their future by luck; they create their own luck through belief and use action to invent it. Our vision and the belief that we associate with it determine what our future will be and its realization. To give our future the best possible chance, we will need to strengthen our belief toward our vision. Eleanor Roosevelt once said, *"The future belongs to those who believe in the beauty of their dreams."*

Being optimistic about our vision will influence our daily activities with strategic future plans and enable us to channel our energy toward continuous development for our future realization. Having ultra-precise belief in our vision will give us the ability to invent it by reprogramming our habits and the way we do things. Our vision positions who we want to be by allowing our beliefs to solidify its authenticity. Simply believing in your vision alone will not secure its achievement; you must also define a strategy to materialize it through unstoppable action. Remember, action is the weapon for creating the reality of our belief.

Define a Strategy for Achieving Your Vision

"I believe that people make their own luck by great preparation and good strategy."

- Jack Canfield

Strategy plays a crucial role in making our vision a reality. It is one thing to have a vision; it is another thing to have a define strategy to achieve it. Strategy describes how we are going to get things done. There is absolutely zero chance of achieving a vision without a game plan. A coherent strategy takes you from the unknown to a known destination. Having good strategy is like setting a proper route with a road map to reach one's destination. It prevents you from deviation from your original plan. Though plans can change along the way, the expected outcome is still in its originality. Visionaries begin their mission with the end in mind. Strategy, which is the technical know-how, provides us with a current blue print that makes the vision accomplishment measurable and time-bound.

To achieve our vision in life, we need to set a strategy that will guide us on how to go about fulfilling our unlimited greatness. We have to sit down on a regular basis and create a breakdown structure with priorities on how and when each of the activities will be completed. The old saying *"You get what is planned for"* is a statement of truth that aligns with the science of achievement. Dividing these activities into manageable steps gives us the opportunity to think through the process of achieving each and every one of these set goals. Vision achievement requires ample planning so as to know what resource is required to drive our mission to birth the possibility of our vision. Strategy is one of the mechanics that the extraordinary people established and used for accomplishing their life mission.

"Vision gets the dream started and defined strategy makes it happen."
-Ayo Jimmy

South African-born Los Angeles entrepreneur Elon Musk, who started learning how to program at the age of nine and sold his first video game that he coded at the age of twelve for $500, said he dedicated his child hood spare time to thinking and drawing up strategy on how to revolutionize the world. After a rough South African upbringing, this insanely ambitious goal-getter used defined strategy to transform his vision into a concrete reality. He helped create Zip2 and PayPal. Musk believes that humanity needs to expand their limits of consciousness to set their future strategy, and asking the right questions was the password that led to his building of a multibillion-dollar fortune companies that make electric cars, solar panels and launch rockets into space. To involve ourselves in the act of defining daily strategy that will lead us to the achievement of our date with destiny, there are certain characteristic that we must aligned to. Chapter Five of this book describes the must-dos that we can major in to define effective strategy for our future. See Embrace the habit of taking action.

Effectively Manage Your Time
to Fulfill Your Vision

"I am aware that success is more than a good idea. It is timing too."
-Anita Roddick

It doesn't matter how we slice it. Knowing that we all have 24 hours in day, seven days a week, four weeks in a month and 365 days in a year is essential to effective planning and management of each and every day of our life without wasting the most essential resource that we have in our possession. Time is an irreplaceable resource. How we use our time helps determine the distance that we will travel on our journey to greatness. Our life is a package with sequences of choices and decisions that revolve around time. Understanding the value of our time equips us with the ability to succeed where others fail.

Effective management of our time is a commitment that is accounted for by what we produce with the little time we have in our hands. By effectively managing our time we can eliminate the pressure that comes from the "I don't have enough time" syndrome. Using each second, minute and hour of each day wisely is important. Since *"time and tide wait for no man."* The allocation of our time daily to working toward our life vision is a psychological discipline that we all have to place into our busy schedules when we plan our daily activities.

We need to adopt values that are consistent with the effective management of our time to fulfill our vision. Asking ourselves which activity is more important and how much time should be assigned to its achievement is paramount on our adventure to abundant life. We must give ourselves permission to work hard toward the accomplishment of our dream by blocking out some hours daily to complete simple tasks that will lead us to the achievement of our greater vision. It's a very logical belief that having effective control of our time improves our decision-making ability and enables us to accomplish more with less effort. Steve Chandler uses the image of a swordsman in his book **Time Warrior** as a metaphor to elaborate more on the power of effective time management. The extraordinary people are time negotiators who adopt the time-chunking techniques to their daily activities.

"Time is money but very few people know how to spend it wisely."

-*Ayo Jimmy*

Lisa Nichols is a media personality and corporate CEO whose global platform has reached and served nearly 30 million people who have used her effective time management psychological discipline to master the art of living a purposeful life. She advanced from being a public assistant to running a multimillionaire dollar public company. On Inside Quest talk show with Tom Bilyeu, Lisa expressed how spending her time wisely led to her life transformation. While working at Los Angeles Unified School District she knew she couldn't stay there because the role she was employed for required a degree and she didn't have one. She made a commitment to herself to be her own rescue. Lisa put a time-chunking technique in place and started to manage her time to attend conferences and lectures on entrepreneurship and brand creation. She gave herself permission to succeed by allocating her after-work hours daily to self-develop and educate herself while building her business at the same time.

According Lisa, she would put her son in the day care during the day and pick him up after nine hours work daily. She would only take 30 minutes before starting work on her personal development from 6:30 in the afternoon till mid night every day. Understanding the value of time and how to use it to her own advantage helped her to become the most sought-after transformational female speaker in the world today. Create a plan to use your time to buy your freedom.

"Time not well used can never be retrieved; don't allow yourself to be a victim of time. Plan your life!"

-*Ayo Jimmy*

Your Vision is not for Sale

"Until we realise that our dream is priceless, we will continue to help others harness their destiny."

-*Ayo Jimmy*

Our ability to hold firm to our vision and know within us that it has no price tag is key. As we grow in life we get trapped by distractions that force us to doubt our ultimate life mission and offer it for sale at a cheaper price. We stop pursuing our vision because we get too comfortable with our good life, which was offered to us by others. We become complacent with a life of comfort instead of stretching out and reaching for greatness. Apparently, the obstacle that stands between us and our vision is not because we don't believe in its achievement. It's because we allow others to influence our decision and place a price tag on our priceless vision. We offer our intention to follow our dream to our boss, family members and friends and they promise us good fortune by increasing our value and potential which they have previously capped because it will enable them to fulfil their own future which they believe you are to help them harness directly or indirectly. Once this happens we cage ourselves in our comfort zone and become reluctant to step outside our life of comfort and strive fearlessly for our life of abundance. We close the chapter on our goal achievement and never allow who we truly are to see the light of the day. We sell out our potential that is worth more than silver and gold for pay raises and bogus welfare packages.

Visions are meant to be birthed by a visionary; they are not a product that should be offered for sale because others don't believe in their reality or because they felt you could be manipulated to trade your worth for a financial value. Why is it a coincidence that when we are about to start chasing our vision good opportunities arrive at our doorsteps to prevent us from taking the step of faith on our life ambition? The only response to that is because the enemy of the best is the good. We allow people to keep us under their control at the expense of fulfilling our vision in the name of working to make a living and not designing a life.

Good opportunities are used as a weapon by others to negotiate for our vision, hoping we will offer it for sale. Their intent is to buy us out of our dreams if we agree not to spread our wings and follow the best version of ourselves by continuously working toward their goals. That is why many people are still stuck in the corporate world today. They want to chase their dream but they feel they are not worthy of their vision so they trade it out to help their companies and bosses achieve their goals for life. Your vision is not a sellable product. It is what we need to accomplish through struggle and pain so that the world can feel the reason why we exist on this planet. No matter what happens to you in life, don't sell out your vision for transient pleasure. It is worth more than the price they offer for it. Listen to your inner calling.

"Chase the vision, not the money, and the money will end up following you."

-Tony Hsieh

This illuminating and inspiring story from Officechai, an online magazine, reflects on how this visionary ditched her bigger paycheck, cushy secure job and stable life style for an uncertain future and financial instability because she realised that her vision is priceless.

Upasana Makati, who was working as a PR agency in Mumbai, had that light bulb moment and decided to quit her job because she no longer wanted to be a corporate slave. Upasana, who wondered about the reading options for the visually impaired and could not see any in her environment before she decided to create White Print, India's first English lifestyle magazine in Braille, says, "There is nothing more satisfying than giving a shape to one's dream."

Despite all the hurdles, from the right legal procedure to advertising challenges, getting the title of the magazine approved after two rejections and eight long months and creating awareness of the magazine in the visually impaired community, Upasana strongly convinced herself that her brainchild was a step in the right direction. Today White Print magazine is powered by over 500 contributors from various professions and age groups who are taking action every day to help visually impaired citizens in India to engage and acquire knowledge that will help transform their lives.

"You get paid for your labour not your vision; follow your life's ambition. Life is too short."

-Ayo Jimmy

QUICK REFLECTION

1. Describe in your own words why it is very important to define your vision.

2. What are four key lessons that you have learned from this chapter?

3. Mention two reasons why you think defining a strategy for the achievement of your vision is key to your success.

4. What are some of the simple steps that you can follow to discover your "WHY"?

5. Based on your assessment of your current situation, list two important reasons why you must document your vision and list two ways to document your vision.

6. After reading this chapter can you explain in your own words why you think belief is essential to the achievement of your vision?

7. Why do you think time management is important? Identify five ways to use your time effectively to enhance the achievement of your vision.

CHAPTER 2

THE POWER OF VISUALIZATION

"If you want to reach a goal, you must see the reaching in your own mind before you actually arrive at your goal."

-Zig Ziglar

Visualizing what we want to achieve is one of the most powerful methods that we can use to help us in making our vision happen. It is a powerful mind technique that we must master on our journey to greatness because it will enable us to consistently envision the reality of our desire. The art of visualizing the reality of our vision before it materializes empowers us with enormous courage and determination to chase its achievement without any delay or procrastination. When our mind thinks it already has what we are imagining and we create that emotional connection to the imagery, it will attract it into our lives. Visualization creates clear, vivid pictures that focus our attention to the possibility of the realization of our vision. It is the power of manifestation in infographic form that turns our optimism into reality by reprogramming our subconscious mind. Mental imagination can be used to prepare for any kinds activities.

Research has shown that this conscious process of creating image in the mind has been used by successful entrepreneurs, business magnates, actors and athletes to unlock their passion, improve their performance and create their desired outcomes. On Oprah Winfrey show Jim Carey, a famous actor and comedian, credits his constant visualization at night on Mulholland drive to the achievement of a $10 million contract which he wrote himself a belief check for in 1985. Using this mental imaginative instrument will shape our belief about who we are and improve our self-esteem. If we consistently visualize the attainment of our vision our subconscious mind goes to work to ensure its actualization by getting us closer daily to the realization of that vision. Visualizing results is actually a practice that coordinates the training of our subconscious mind to stimulate our reticular activating system to help accomplish our vision. Brain research evidence reveals that imagination through mental instruction propels unstoppable action. Creating the vision of who you want to become and living in that picture through visualization will accelerate the achievement of your ambition. It will line up your subconscious with activities and create that innate motivation to make big things happen in your life.

The daily practice of mental rehearsal, of seeing our vision as already complete, will rapidly accelerate the achievement of our ambitions by conditioning our neural pathway to create a scenario that makes action feel familiar to physical performance. Visualization practice has given so many higher achievers super power to accomplish their dreams through the law of attraction. Why should we visualize our vision before its fulfillment? Aside from the fact that envisioning the success of our vision can enhance motivation and confidence to act, it will open our eyes to ways and steps to follow in achieving our desire. According to Tom Seabourne, the author of The Complete Idiot's Guide to Quick Total Body Workout, visualization cannot make us perform beyond our ability but it can help us tap into our unlimited potential.

> "Whatever the mind of man can conceive and believe,
> it can achieve."
>
> -Napoleon Hill

Jack Nicklaus, who happens to be the greatest ever golfer, recognized the power of visualization. This iconic legend of golf nicknamed the Golden Bear because of his skills and indisputable potential, is widely regarded as the greatest golfer of all time due to his unbeatable record of 18 professional major championships while producing 19 second place and 9 third place finishes over a span of 25 years. Jack Nicklaus, one of the sport messiahs that helped transform golf during his playing days, said he never hit a shot, not even in practice, without having a very sharp in-focus picture of it in his mind. In his statement, he mentioned that always he will first visualize the ball where he wanted it to finish before he takes a swing that will turn the image into reality. His belief in the power of visualization is backed up by philosophy, which shows that an effective shot in golf is 10% swing, 40% setup and 50% mental picture of the optimal swing.

Holding the mental picture of one's vision long and steady enough in one's subconscious mind will program the brain to recognize resources, people and circumstances that will help achieve the dream. It will also build the intrinsic motivation to actualize the vision. Even though visualization is a common occurrence in most people's lives, to be able to do it regularly will require practice. Constant practice of this mental workout will not only stimulate the sympathetic nervous system, which governs our fight or flight mood, it will also help us to get better in the act. Relaxation, reinforcement and regularity are some of the key elements that enhance effective visualization. If you are currently looking for ways to develop and apply powerful visualization skills, here are some of the proven techniques that you can use to improve ways of visualizing your results.

1. Write Down what you want to Visualize

To create a mental image of a future event we must first have an idea of what we are aiming to achieve. As the author of The Mental Athlete Kay Porter said, *"If we want to hone our effort we must put the story of how it will unfold in writing."* Writing down in detail what we want to visualize will not only give us a plan to fall back on, but it will also enable us to envision each action necessary before the achievement of the outcome. The writing statement allows the mind to take a photograph of the natural scenery and embed it into our imagination so that we can see the future event as if it's happening and not as if we are wishing it would happen in the future.

It is very important that we write down what we want to visualize because it will help us to create vivid mental images and increase our chances of achieving them. Jack Canfield, the author of Chicken Soup for the Soul, talked about how writing his goal in relation to Chicken Soup for the Soul on a 3x5 index card and reading through these stacks of cards each morning and night before closing his eyes to visualize the completion of that goal in its perfect state for about 15 seconds has helped move the book to number one in paperback advice and one of the most popular and loved books ever published. We can enhance the accomplishment of our desired future by sketching it in detail on paper.

2. Focus on Details

Having the ability to stay focused is crucial for every activity that we engage in but sometimes we lose it just when we need it the most. Focusing on details during visualization can help one think constructively about the importance of the message and how it can be accomplished without any distortion from fear or situation within our environment. Allowing our mind to focus without interruption will create vivid scenarios that will give us that innate confidence with unshakeable belief that our imagination is real and achievable. David Rock, author of Your Brain at Work, states that twenty minutes a day of deep focus is highly transformative. His statement was affirmed by viable research evidence, which shows that if we engage the 18 billion brain cells in our brain and get them all working in a singular direction for the creation of our life plan, the imagery will definitely empower our ability to create them. Using this technique in the course of visualization will activate our creative subconscious mind and start to draw into our life resources, people and circumstances that will enhance our ability to materialize our imagination.

The extraordinary power of our subconscious mind can be harnessed if we stay focus on the details of our life event and conduct daily rituals of practice to establish the right balance. To effectively focus on the details of our life event during visualization we most turn off all distractions by practicing concentration. Focusing requires a lot of willpower and for us to perfect this act during visualization we can do any of the following:

- Pick a consistent focus spot for our visualization ritual
- Design focusing hours for visualization daily
- Stare at a distant object for a few minutes

3. Consistent Practice

If we struggle with visualization, consistent practice is one of the areas that we need to critically look into to help shape our visualization pattern. Effective mental rehearsing is wishful thinking and everyone has the ability to envision, but to enhance this ability we will need to engross ourselves in regular practice. It doesn't matter if our ability to visualize is weak at the outset. Visualization is a skill that we can all get better at but like anything else it requires regular practice. Ten minutes every day will create the momentum and make commitment to practicing visualization easy. It will develop and strengthen our ability to train the mind to master the mental image of future events and interpret imagery as equivalent to a real-life action. According to Matt Neason, a leading Australian Peak Performance Consultant and founder of Peak Performance Sports, *"Regular practice of visualization creates powerful feelings that bridge the gap between the performance at peak in the mind and performance at peak in the real world.*

Constant connection with the picture in our subconscious mind will enable us to nurture our vision and allow the drive for its achievement to grow. Consistent practice of visualization will increase our chances of success and help us gain inner strength with self-confidence if we master the act effectively.

"Our lives are what our thoughts make them."

-Marcus Aurelius

The Importance of Visualization

Visualization creates the pattern through which all future achievement will emerge by making mental images. The construction of any building starts with the architect's visualization of the magnificent structure, as does the creation of our future desire. To materialize the existence of our dream we have to create the mental picture of its attainment. Here are some of the benefits that you will experience when you practice visualization.

❖ **You will be stress free**

When we adopt the principle of visualizing our vision, the mind associates the sensation of relaxation with peaceful images. Constant visualization introduces an element of distraction which often serves as a redirection to draw our attention away from what is stressing us toward an alternative focus. According to Dr. Michael Breus, the act of rehearsing mental imagery can help reduce stress by causing a relaxation response in the muscles and that triggers the sensation that builds a peaceful, calm and joyful mood for the individual. Practicing visualization will help diffuse tense moments by detaching us from moment-to-moment fixation on the contents of our minds and cultivating a relaxed sensation with positive thoughts streaming through the mind.

Visualization opens a channel for us to transform our stressful thoughts into a greater degree of relaxation with positive perception from guided imagery. Diane Tusek, former director of the Guided Imagery Program at the Cleveland Clinic, researched evidence that patients who imbibed the culture of using guided imagery were more relaxed, needed less pain medication and went home from the hospital sooner than their peers who did not. Visualization practice will help to eliminate stress and reduce the severity of headaches by strengthening immune function. This technique offers an opportunity for stress reduction but if we want to gain the results we must commit a significant amount of our time daily to practicing mental imagery.

❖ **You will have constant Joy**

Buddhist monk and peace activist Thich Nhat Hanh said, *"Sometimes our joy is the source of our smile, but sometime our smile can be the source of our joy."* Visualization practicing can enable us to use the power of our imagination to recall mindful things that will bring us constant joy. Focusing on the mental imagery in our subconscious mindset aligns clarity with positive belief, which induces strong feelings of joy. Spending more time in the feelings of joy that the mental picture creates will boost our confidence and enable us to use this powerful force to actualize the realization of our vision by erasing our self-limiting thoughts.

There is no limit to our imagination. If you visualize yourself earning seven figures and creating your own business from scratch like I did when I left the army three years ago, you will be able to manifest your vision into reality. While visualization works, I would like to quickly point out to you at this point that it also requires an element of action. Visualization will not make things appear miraculously out of nothingness because it is not magic. Instead it will help you to lay the foundation for the accomplishment of your vision by creating the right mental belief and attitude that will enhance your ability to do what is necessary to achieve your desire. This is where the constant inducement of the strong feeling of joy emanates from.

❖ **You will increase yourself-confidence**

How we react to circumstances in our life depends greatly on how confident we are and the philosophy we hold about the situation. These two elements define our character because they are associated with our self-image. Our mind will only present what it believes to be the solution to our current situation. An experiment that involves two individuals that have never played basketball before in their life was conducted by a researcher to verify if our subconscious brain can tell the difference between real life and imaginary events. These two individuals were asked to shoot 20 balls each on a basketball court. At the end of the 20 shots both guys performed badly and could not even make a basket. The researcher asked these two individuals to go back home and return in two weeks' time for a reshot. Before departing on their way, he told one of them to practice visualizing himself shooting the ball through the hoop until the action became familiar to his brain and asked the second lad to come the following week without rehearsing any form of mental imagery.

The research evidence proved that the guy that was asked to practice visualization was more confident and on target in shooting the ball through the hoop than the second lad that did not visualize. Constant practice of visualization not only strengthens our chance of success it also creates peace of mind with inner joy that boosts our self-esteem and self-confidence. The reality of it all is that when you repeatedly visualize your vision you are tricking the brain into believing it is real and once it does, it will surely activate many of the same neural pathways in the brain that will play it out as real. Practicing constant visualization will help externalize our visions and make them real.

❖ **You will improve your performance**

A huge part of achieving any dream lies in our ability to visualize it. Brain studies revealed that thoughts produce the same mental instruction as actions. What we think about projects the reality of what we will create. Regular practice of visualization enhances performance and increases motivation. Many athletes find imagery helpful in elevating their performance because it allows them to mentally practice competing against specific opponents. Visualization practice allows us to create multisensory simulation of ourselves executing the act.

By mastering the movement in our head and familiarizing ourselves with the accompanied sensation, our body is primed to achieve a peak performance when we take action. Natan Sharansky, a famous former Soviet refusnik and human right activist that was convicted of treason and spying on behalf of the United States by the USSR implemented the principle of visualization during his nine-year jail term. While in solitary confinement Sharansky played mental chess, which enable him to become a world champion in chess. In 1996, this technique enabled Sharansky to defeat the world champion chess player Garry Kasparov.

Constant practicing of mental imagery triggers areas of the brain that will activate the muscles and improves our strength to reach peak performance in whatever we do. So, keep your regular practice of mental imagery to improve your performance beyond expectations.

❖ You will materialize your dream

One of the most powerful effect of good visualization practice is that it rekindles our drive to manifest our innermost desires. The more we are mentally rehearsing what we want to achieve, the faster our brain looks for ways to make it happen in real life. According to Dr. Bruno Roque Cignacco, the author of *How to Manifest Money Effortlessly*, our thought has a specific vibration, either good or bad. When we hold these positive images in our subconscious mind we are radiating positive vibration to enhance our ability to create it reality.

Constant practice of visualizing our innate desires, couple with massive action, will empower our real self to cultivate a deeper connection that will intensify our ability to materialize our dreams. Lindsey Vonn, one of the most successful female skiers in American history, revealed how she has been able to use consistent practice of mental imagery to materialize her Olympic dream during an interview with *MindBodyGreen*. Vonn commented that she always visualizes the run before she does it and by the time she gets to the start gate she has already run that race 100 times in her head, with a vivid picture of how it will be achieved. Doing that always inflames her strength to materialize the dream. While visualization techniques and practices are definitely true, it is highly essential that they are properly implemented and backed up with actions.

"To accomplish great things we must first dream, then visualize, then plan ... believe ... act."

-Alfred A Montapert

QUICK REFLECTION

1. In this chapter, we explored visualization in detail. Why do you think is it important to visualize?

2. Which of the visualization habits mentioned in the book do you think you can develop over time to help you improve your ability to transform your life? List three areas of your life where you can use visualization techniques to manifest its outcome.

3. What are the lessons that you picked out from the stories of the extraordinary people mentioned in this chapter?

CHAPTER 3

CURIOSITY EMPOWERS GENIUSITY

"Desire is the seed plot of all human greatness, as curiosity is the bedrock of all innovations."

-Ayo Jimmy

If you aren't curious about the world, it is probably because you think there are no interesting things that you haven't yet discovered. There is one factor that sets apart the extraordinary from the ordinary. It is their desire to learn. Curiosity is the trait that separates our thoughts from our emotions. It is what the great minds of the world call the heart of lifelong learning that gives birth to creativity. The hidden force that drives the heart of learning lies in curiosity. Cultivating inquisitiveness is the joy of exploration that encompasses reasoning and critical thinking. Curiosity has been the major impetus behind scientific discoveries and the advancement of civilization. It helps us approach uncertainty in our everyday lives with a positive attitude. The great inventors of the world, such as Thomas Edison, Richard Feynman, Leonardo da Vinci and Steve Jobs, are all known for their adventures which came from their curiosity. According to George Mason University Professor Todd Kashdan, the author of *Curious? Discover the*

41

Missing Ingredient to Fulfilling Life, **"Curiosity is nothing more than what we feel when we are struck by something novel."** It is a mental state that allows us to be extraordinarily interested in something different from what we already know.

The life of a curious person is far from being boring because there are always new things that will attract their attention. Curious people are explorers that actively look for challenges that will stretch their boundaries. Albert Einstein was born in Ulm Wurttemberg in Germany on March 14, 1879 to a Jewish family. During his elementary school days at the Luitpold Gymnasium in Munich he struggled with the institution's rigid pedagogical style because he had what was considered to be speech and writing challenges, another word for dyslexia. Albert's youth was marked by deep inquisitiveness, which helped him with his passion for playing violin and writing his first paper, *The state of Aether in Magnetic field.* After graduating from Swiss Polytechnic Albert had a hard time finding employment and he tried to apply for multiple academic positions which he was turned down for. He eventually found steady work in 1902 after receiving a referral for a clerk position in the Swiss patent office. While working at the patent office Albert had the time to further explore his curiosity on ideas that had taken hold during his studies at Polytechnic. In 1905 Albert was struck by novelty which ignited his potential to publish his four papers: *"Brownian motion, Photoelectric effect, matter and energy relationship and special theory of relativity,"* which took physics in a new and electrifying direction. His curiosity led to the fundamental laws of physics which birthed most of the modern inventions that we are using today: the lasers and the telecommunication system, which includes cell phone and satellites. Today Albert Einstein is not only one of the most important physicist in history, his personality and fame have made him a cultural icon as well, so much so that Time Magazine named him the person of the century. Einstein's work influenced the world and philosophy of science because of his heart of curiosity. Our state of curiosity will determine how much and how far we can get in life. *It takes consistency to create winning in any endeavor but what separates the extraordinary from the ordinary is their childlike curiosity.*

Extraordinary people seek to understand by asking questions that start with "how," "what," "when," "where" and "why". This, according to experts, is the key to their greatness. Each of us is born with the gift of curiosity about the world around us but as we grow older we stop seeking and asking questions that fill us with this insatiable wonder because of our fear, doubt, shame and the opinions of others about us. Steve Jobs, the inventor and industrial designer of game changing-products that rule the world, understood the power of curiosity as the heart of innovation. According to Steve, much of what he stumbled into that turned out to be the priceless products of today came from following up on his childlike curiosity.

The key fact about life is that the great idea that will enhance our ability to fulfill our desire is in our thought process; all we need to do is to start seeking and searching by putting curiosity at the heart of everything we do. Take few minutes to ponder on these questions; where do you want to be and what idea will get you there? Asking yourselves these rhetorical questions will not only enable you to harness your dream; it will also unearth the trajectory that you want to follow. International bestselling author Bryant McGill said, *"Curiosity is one of the great secrets of happiness."* Cultivating our childlike curiosity will set us apart from people that are merely surviving and provide us with the opportunity to materialize our unlimited potential. Here are some of the game changing habits practiced by incredibly curious people.

❖ **They Ask Questions Relentlessly**

Our minds have two halves; one half acquire experiences and the other half interprets and creates understanding of those experiences. Curious people use both halves of their minds and are able to stretch them to new height by constantly asking questions to gain clarity. They embrace asking lots of questions because it empowers them with the ability to become familiar with the unfamiliar. Engaging in regular questioning takes our mind from being passive into an active mode. Professor Michael Marquardt, the author of Leading with Questions, famously said, *"Questions wake people up. They prompt new ideas. They show people new places and new ways of doing things."*

Asking questions creates openness for both the person who is being asked and the person who is asking for meaningful clarity. Research studies have proven time and time again that maintaining a healthy level of curiosity about different viewpoints enables people to maintain social relationships. Asking questions relentlessly will not only help us discover new ideas; it will also open up new possibilities.

❖ **They Constantly seeking for Knowledge**

Curious people are active mentally because they have an innate desire to dig deeper until their thirst for answers is quenched. They seek new knowledge by reading, researching and engaging in conversations. Aside from the fact that curious individuals develop an excessive love for learning, they are novelty seekers that are always dissatisfied with the status quo and are willing to challenge established practices. Curious people are avid learners that cherish gathering of knowledge with higher emphasis on wisdom and clarity in all things. Leonardo Da Vinci was best known for his love for knowledge seeking. His life was filled with exciting experiments, some of which were the opening of corpses to learn how the human body functions and the observation of the flow of water to create mechanics.

Constant learning can cause changes in the brain chemistry to help us retain life transforming information. New research by a team of US-based psychologists at the University of California revealed that our mind actively rewards us for seeking out new information in our most interested area. To cultivate our curious mind, we must be coachable and open to learning with unlearning. We must be ready to look at life through excitement lenses and enjoy the learning process.

❖ **They are not afraid to admit that they don't know**

Passionately curious people not only express interest in wanting to know more about something; they embrace what they don't know and they are not afraid to admit when they don't have all the answers. They stick around until they get to the bottom of the problem. According to Sue Heilbronner, the *cofounder of MergeLane*, <u>the ability to shelve a sense of being right in favour of being open to other people's opinions is a trait that is commonly natural to curious people</u>. When most folks are afraid of what lies ahead, curious individuals will boldly move forward and take on new challenges that lie before them because they see it as an avenue to discover something new.

Evidence from Harvard psychologist Ellen Langer reveals that curious people are always anxiously waiting for their opportunity to move forward and create something new. They cultivate a sense of being open to others' insights and opinions rather than being right. As wisely affirmed by Socrates, *"I know nothing except the fact of my ignorance."* Curious people follow their values and they are generally less affected by peer pressure. The key question now is: when precisely have you ever admitted to your friends and family that you don't have all the answers to life's questions? Acknowledging that we don't know enough to be a pessimist will stimulate our curiosity to learn something new and be innovative.

❖ They live to solve problems

Curious people are problem solvers because they are keen to learn what they don't know and use it to create new concepts. No matter what the situation is, naturally curious people find something interesting to explore. Their passion for investigating something new fosters their intellectual investment and knowledge acquisition over time. Individuals with strong curiosity traits are more proactive at exploring opportunities; they take risks and turn creative ideas into innovations. They focus more on understanding how and why things work, find creative ways to address some particular issues and create systems that will enable them to solve long-term difficult problems.

Their insatiable urge for knowledge puts them through experimentation processes for new techniques. Pranav Mistry's *TED.com idea worth spreading potential of SixthSense technology* is an amazing story that revealed the natural curiosity of a problem-solving genius who created some of the most entertaining and thought-provoking interfaces that the world had ever seen. Pranav's quest to understand how our everyday knowledge about how objects can be used to help us interact with the digital world led to the creation of intelligent sticky notes (Quickies) that can search and send reminders; a pen that draws in 3D and a tangible public map that can act as the Google of physical worlds with the legendary SixthSense, which is now open-sourced. Imagine how boring life would be if we just didn't care about learning or asking a plethora questions that would lead us to some problem-solving techniques. Don't kill your innate curiosity; it is critical to your life transformation.

The Not So Hidden Genius

From a college dropout to the head of a multi-billion apply empire before his death, Steve Jobs' dramatic transformation of the worlds of personal computing, music and mobile phones is one of the intriguing stories that illustrate the power of a curious mind. Steve's interest in gadgetry and electronics led him to call William Hewlett, the co-founder and president of Hewlett Packard, for information about the missing parts which he discovered when assembling the frequency counter for his eight-grade school project assignment.

The call not only provided Steve with the opportunity of getting the missing parts, William Hewlett also offered Steve a summer internship at Hewlett Packard. During this summer internship program Steve met and befriended Steve Wozniak, a young engineer who had a penchant for tinkering. Steve Job enrolled in Reed College in Portland after his graduation from high school but his voracious curiosity for knowledge was way beyond the conventional educational system so he dropped out of school after one semester. Steve's insatiable curiosity led him to the discovery of books on Shakespeare, Dylan Thomas and the classic literary stuff, which prompted him to start attending a calligraphy course taught by Robert Palladino as an unofficial student in Reed College.

His early life was filled with confusion and chaos. Steve faced several issues in his life, to the extent that he travelled to India with friends in search of enlightenment. At age twenty Steve Jobs and Steve Wozniak started a company together in a garage in April 1976, after Steve Jobs saw a computer that Wozniak designed for himself. Steve Jobs named the company Apple in memory of a happy summer he had spent as an orchard worker in Oregon. Working out of his dad's garage Steve faced a lot of negative comments from people in his neighborhood. Later that year was the birth of the company's first computer, Apple I, which was followed by Apple II, a highly successful mass-produced microcomputer product and the first consumer product that become the best-selling computer in the 70s and 80s.

Curiosity turned out to be Steve's major area of creativity; in 1985, he began a new hardware and software enterprise called NexT Inc. Unsatisfied with his level of knowledge in the field of gadgetry and electronics, Steve purchased an animation company from George Lucas and the animation company later became Pixar Animation Studio, which is popularly known for its production of animated firms such as "The Incredibles" and "Tony Sony." According to Investopedia, at the time of Steve's death in 2011 he had a net worth of $10.2 billion with an estate estimated to be worth over $19 billion 2015. Steve Jobs' willingness to keep solving the world's problems and constant seeking of knowledge by being hyper-curios made him one of the greatest iconoclasts to touch the ugly world of technology and make it beautiful. The key takeaway from this story is that we all have the ability to create who we want to become and leave our mark on Earth but that depends entirely on our willingness to venture into the unknown and explore knowledge that will help us actualize the greatness that we have always dreamed about.

The importance of cultivating curiosity

We are hardwired with the innate desire to solve problems like Pranav Mistry, but we allow fear and faithlessness with the hustling and bustling of life to make us uninterested in finding out the "whys and hows" of life. Being curious will help us in so many ways to approach life's challenges and see possibilities where others see the end of the road. Writer, activist and speaker Bryant H. McGill once said, "Curiosity is one of the great secrets of happiness." Exercising our innate sense of curiosity will create an openness to unfamiliar experiences and lay the groundwork for greater opportunities that will lead to our happiness.

Being inquisitive about everything in our surroundings will make us the true winner that we were born to be and help us shape our behaviours and habits toward what we want to accomplish in life. If you want to keep moving forward, be it in your career, academic pursuit, personal development, business or physical fitness, curiosity is an important attribute that you need to possess. Here are some of the reasons why cultivating our curiosity is essential to our progress in life.

❖ **It improves our level of intelligence**

Developing our curiosity will make the mind observant and active. It will brighten our ability to view things differently with the possibility of discovering the hidden secret of innovation and ways through which we can create viable solutions to our problems. The mental exercise that we will experience as a result of being curious will not only strengthen our level of intelligence, it will stimulate our mind by liberating our creative emotion and thought from the tension of daily routine. As writer Thomas Hobbes once expressed, "Curiosity is the lust of the mind."

Cultivating our curiosity will equip us with a wealth of knowledge that will help us in making the right decisions that will lead us to breakthroughs and new opportunities. Constantly seeking out novel activities and gaining new experience through mind engagement will increase our IQ and expand our cognitive horizons. People who are actively exhibiting their inquisitiveness always experience higher levels of satisfaction and find a greater sense of meaning in life. You have unlimited potential to create your own greatness and for you to harness this potential, you will need to continuously challenge yourself by developing your curiosity. Engage yourself in purposeful practices.

❖ **It creates authentic happiness**

We all want to be happy; according to Dalai Lama, the holiness guru and spiritual leader *"Happiness is the very purpose of our life."* We are all capable of achieving happiness and more meaning in life if we adopt the right attitude, which is to engineer our intellectual ability. Finding happiness in life does not just feel good but it increases our ability to grow physically and improve our financial status. The fever for happiness can be spurred through the enrichment of our intense desire to know. Research evidence on the neuroplasticity of our brain reveals that happiness, compassion and kindness are traits of life that we can enhance through the development of our curiosity.

Exercising our innate sense of curiosity will eliminate boredom and give our minds opportunities to grow. It will kindle our happiness and joy by putting us in a position to boost our creative thinking ability through learning about topics that engross our interest. Developing our curiosity is one of the key elements that could help us live life at its fullest if we follow it properly and consistently. One thing is certain; if we want to continuously improve our level of happiness in any areas of our life we must focus more on cultivating our curiosity so as to tap into the great power that lies within us.

❖ **It enhances effectiveness in social relationships**

Nurturing our sense of curiosity is the social glue that strengthens our relationships and creates a better connection with others over time, if we improve on it. By actively enhancing our curiosity we are naturally increasing the quality of our life experience and relationships. According to Anthony Robbins, the personal development icon and strategist for success, "The quality of our life is in direct proportion to the quality of our relationships." Cultivating our curiosity by asking questions during social gatherings and engaging in heart-to-heart conversions will strengthen our desire for learning and foster our level of intimacy whenever we meet with people of different ages and sizes. It will help navigate our happiness and enrich our lives with fun. Studies have proven that people who are passionately curious are more engaged and socially interactive.

Curiosity always opens up dialogue that will increase an achievement-driven relationship and greater satisfaction between parties if it is well developed and implemented during social engagement. To have a successful relationship, either at home with our family or at work with our colleagues we must develop the habit of curiosity on regular basis. The degree to which we cultivate our curiosity will directly or indirectly impact our personal growth, opportunities and relationships. Setting aside time to continuously develop your sense of curiosity will enable you to create an overall life of fulfillment and happiness.

Building our Curiosity

Developing our curiosity is one of the amazing characteristics that can help shape and remodel our philosophy about life and the environment that we live in. For us to unleash our curiosity we must be willing to learn and unlearn. In fact, we must keep learning and experimenting with new ideas to expand our perspective and field of awareness. Cultivating our sense of curiosity through learning will intrinsically motivate our innate desire for knowledge. George Freud Lowenstein, an American educator and economist, once said, *"When our attention becomes focused on a gap in our knowledge, such an information gap produce the feeling of curiosity."* Curiosity is one of the most superficial of all affections that changes the curious perpetually because it has that inexplicable itch that tell us to keep looking for answers to the unknown. The more curiosity we can muster the more life-transforming information we will have access to. If you are willing to boost your ability to think creatively, here are some steps that you can apply.

❖ **Be interested in everything**

Change can be a little scary when we are used to routines that we don't even have to think about, but for us to grow our mind we must be ready to explore the power of curiosity by showing interest in everything. We must read two to three pages in books with topics of interest daily and research key activities that we are passionate about. Having a breadth of knowledge in diverse fields is very valuable to our life transformation because it will empower us with information that will give us an edge in all areas of life, be it in our business or social life and relationships. To stay intellectually curious, we must be open-minded, ask a plethora of questions and be able to engage in constructive mind discussions with others.

The story of John Lloyd, a writer, TV producer and director, is a great illustration of someone whose immense curiosity led to his idea for the BBC quiz show QI. John Lloyd suffered from depression which brought his headlong career as a producer to an abrupt halt. As depressed people often do, he started to isolate himself from friends and family and lost interest in his daily activities. John's feeling of hopelessness led him to start creating sheer havoc on his family by trying to program everyone's activities and forcing his eight-year-old to do a regular piano practice. John's family eventually told him to stop trying to produce the family as if he was running a TV program. His life-changing moment came when he stopped concentrating on his problems and started channeling his mind toward reading about everything. In his interview with Lesley Garner from *The Telegraph*, John Lloyd said, "I dealt with my depression by simply followed my curiosity, I took time off work, started going on long walks and read voraciously."

His voracious reading with long walks and daily thinking created a new life excitement that restored sanity to him and his family. His quest for knowledge and interest in everything led to his idea for the BBC Two comedy quiz program which now educates audiences. Developing interest everything around us can lead us in a direction of fruitfulness if we are willing to drop everything else and focus on studying the true reality of life.

❖ Embrace Uncertainty

A Writer Brandon A. Trean once said, *"It is how we embrace the uncertainty in our lives that will lead to the great transformation of our souls."* One of the most reliable way to encourage our innate curiosity to ignite our hunger for creative thinking and help turn our daily activities into enjoyable experiences is to embrace uncertainty. You might be wondering why embracing uncertainty is tagged as one of the most reliable ways for building curiosity. Let's quickly do some critical thinking tests which I believe will illuminate this statement. Imagine knowing the results for all the Olympic activities before the start of the events. Would you watch the events when they really started or not? My guess is as good as yours. Knowing these results beforehand would take away the interest, surprise and thrill of watching the game live. Embracing uncertainty creates that state of genuine interest with surprise and tension that tests the prediction of the unknown.

Cultivating our sense of curiosity by diving deep into uncertainty will not only activate our happiness, it will also empower us with the ability to find more meaning in life than people who rely on certainty. The better we become at uncertainty, the easier it becomes to engage our curiosity amidst any ambiguity. To harness our urge for insatiably curiosity it is paramount that we constantly engage in activities where we are uncertain about the outcome.

❖ Seek Clarity

To develop an inquiring mind, we must not only be open to everything, we also need to seriously engage in seeking clarity by asking a plethora of questions. Anthony Robbins, the personal development icon and strategist for success once said *"Clarity is power."* Clarity stimulates questions and questions ignite curiosity. More often than not, we focus more on finding answers rather than seeking clarity by asking genuinely interesting questions that will open an information gap. Questions are the tools that shine the light of clarity on the unknown by priming curiosity. According to Nancy Willard, an American poet and author, *"Sometimes questions are more important than answers."* Kindle devices, iPhones and Dyson vacuum cleaners were born from the act of questioning that is deeply rooted in the quest for clarity.

The brain does not like to have unclear information and because of that it will shift into seeking and finding mode to uncover and understand the unknown. Seeking clarity will change our learning process from something dull to a treasure hunt and give us a chance to solve bigger problems that are itching for creative solutions. We can become an inquisitive explorer of clarity if we are willing to pursue learning by asking essential questions anywhere at any time.

"Every addition to true knowledge is an addition to human power."

-Horace Mann

QUICK REFLECTION

1. Why do you think curiosity is important to the pursuit of an idea that is greatly significant to your life? Identify three reasons why it is important to be curious.

2. According to the stories discussed in this chapter we have seen how curiosity has changed the course of history and led to numerous breakthroughs. List two ways that curiosity can help you improve your creative ability.

3. Think about how you were motivated to learn as a child. What were you curious about then? Identify some of the steps that you can take now to bring back that childlike curiosity.

CHAPTER 4

PROCRASTINATION KILLS DREAMS

"Success has neither mercy for laziness nor pity for procrastination. Don't be casual with your dreams."

-Ayo Jimmy

Edward Young the English writer who wrote *"Procrastination is the thief of time"* must have realized the destructive impact that procrastination has on success actualization. How many times have you heard someone say 'I will do it later'? I believe you would have made the same statement at one point in your life. Yes, we are all guilty of the common human tendency to procrastinate. The main reason we tend to procrastinate is because getting urgent tasks done requires hard work and hard work is something that gets us out of our comfort zone. Procrastination makes us more sensitive to the pleasure of the moment and stops us from concentrating on our long-term goals. Many people procrastinate to some degree but some are chronic procrastinators. When we procrastinate, we are simply refusing to take action on the very things that we know will bring us the rewards that we so desire.

Unfortunately, this self-inflicted disease has assassinated many people's life time opportunities. Wayne Gretzky former

Canadian professional ice hockey player and head coach, said, *Procrastination is one of the most common and deadliest of diseases and its toll on success and happiness is heavy.* It emerges as a result of our lack of self-regulatory ability. Little episodes of procrastination can quickly add up and become the arch enemy of our dreams. Research statistics indicate that as many as 95 percent of people suffer from this addiction. Lack of motivation, fear of failure, excessive workload, laziness and the fear of success are some of the reasons given for this maladaptive behaviour. Professor Clarry Lay, a prominent writer on this subject, said procrastination occurs when there is a temporal gap between intended behaviour and the actual behaviour. It is a way of putting off the inevitable at the expense of short-term gratification for doing nothing. While our reasons for procrastination may differ, the result is often the same: nothing gets done and we hang the guilt of shame over our head.

Our natural response to unpleasant activities in our life is to block them out and focus more on what is convenient and easy for us to do at that time but by putting off the key essentials of our life because they are unpleasant we are trading off our confidence and self-esteem and allowing the events of life to control us. One thing is certain: when procrastination becomes a habit, it makes opportunities difficult for us to notice. It uses the short-term pleasure of free time that it creates as a preventive mechanism to stop us from taking on real challenges that will cause us to evolve outside our comfort zone and take on greater opportunities that require our actions. For us to achieve any viable objective or plans that we set for ourselves in different areas of our life we must create a method of overcoming this self-limiting behaviour.

The Messenger of the Past

I left the army a few years ago and joined the bandwagon of the nine-to-five work force within the project management industry. Writing best-selling books and becoming a publisher was the dream I had nursed in my heart for a long time, but putting the research material together and attending different weekly self-publishing programs with seminars is a process that would require a considerable amount of my time, which was tantamount to me giving up my day job. I became so afraid of leaving my job to go chase my dream because I have a family to feed and a mortgage to pay. Asides from that, I was just settling back into civilian life after spending over seven years of my life serving my nation. I got so overwhelmed with the notion that if I left my job it would become very difficult for me to provide for my family and pay off my mortgage. Although my end goal was clear and it aligned with something I deeply desired, the fear of failure crept in and propelled lack of confidence, which made it uncomfortable for me to resonate with the true belief of who I really wanted to become. I started to procrastinate and convinced myself that the book writing cum becoming a publisher would not work. At some point, I registered for book self-publishing improvement programs and would not attend. I continued to give excuses and hold myself back, and when my vision accountability partner inquired for an update about this goal I would tell her that I needed more time and explain to her that I was still trying to save some money so that I could leave my job and then start the book publishing process.

After spending months moving in circles with excuses why I thought it was not the right time, something happened in my work place and all the contractors were asked to leave, including me. That was when it dawned on me that I had been procrastinating about my future and allowing the messenger of the past to limit me. Instead of going to look for a new job I was adamant to revisit my dream and take my chances. I started attending the book self-publishing improvement programs and along the way I met my mentor, who guided me on how to become a publisher. Four months later I published two quotes books, *Inspiration and wisdom and The Power Words*, that sold over 350 copies and still continue to sell every single day. If hadn't been fired at work I probably wouldn't have started the book writing that led me into having my own publishing company today.

The act of procrastination is literally being selfish to one's tomorrow by enslaving time to laziness. It doesn't just occur with our goals or life changing events. We procrastinate with our everyday activities as well. We waste every precious second of our time doing things that we are not supposed to be doing instead of focusing on key activities that can add benefit to our life. When we avoid doing things that matter and major in minor activities we achieve less and that triggers stress, which results in unhappiness. To create our happiness and accomplish anything tangible in life we must find a way to conquer our delaying and postponing activities.

The Paradox of Procrastination

With the amount of research on procrastination over the last 20 years it's becoming more apparent that procrastination is not just harmful, it's also a mechanism that promotes health problems, anxiety and crises. Chronic procrastination makes people more vulnerable to serious health conditions like hypertension and cardiovascular disease. It is a bad habit that has the ability to rob us of our dreams and abort the plan for greatness in our life if we continuously engage in the act. Mason Cooley, an American aphorist, said, *"Procrastination makes easy things hard and hard things harder."* People who are chronic procrastinators lack willpower and ambition to achieve things. When we delay activities by avoiding obligations we are enhancing a perpetual cycle that will reinforce lack of discipline and loss of precious time. According to online research conducted by the Procrastination Research group at Carleton University in Canada, procrastination causes low self-esteem and it has a negative effect on happiness.

When we avoid doing difficult tasks by postponing them to the next day or the day after it might seem like we are winning by gaining the short-term pleasure of avoiding pain but the consequences of deferring these activities outweigh the pleasures. In addition to the obvious effects of procrastination mentioned above, here are some of the common negative side effects of this limiting behaviour.

❖ **Increases Stress Levels**

The relationship between procrastination and stress is a complicated one. Stress is brought about by high states of arousal in our blood pressure. Our brain is hard wired with an alarm system for protection. When the brain perceives a threat, it signals our body to release a burst of hormones that increase our heart rate and raise our blood pressure. Procrastination creates stress by increasing time pressure when we have considerably less time to complete tasks when the deadline is closer.

At this point we are working at the mercy of long, sleepless nights and stoked with stimulants in order to be able to get the job done. The closer we get to the deadline with the work unaccomplished the more stressed we become. Putting off important tasks can result in greater stress as we rush to ensure that we meet the deadline.

People who procrastinate are more likely to sleep poorly, experience high levels of anxiety, and encounter headaches which can lead to breakdown. You know that you should be working on that project but you can't seem to resist checking through your Facebook, Tweeter feed and friends' pictures on Instagram. Leaving important tasks till the last minute to complete is an unhealthy behaviour that will not only impact your performance but will also affect your health and result in fatigue, discomfort, and burnout. If you are a chronic procrastinator the main thing to remember is to get things done you will have to make the future seem more immediate and act on each activity even when you don't feel like doing it.

❖ **Damaging Reputation**

The effect of procrastination not only causes stress, it can also have negative impact on our image and reputation. When we procrastinate till tomorrow on what we know we should act on today, we are selling ourselves out and that can result in undermining of our personality and physical and mental wellbeing. Chronic procrastination can make people that believe in our potential start to hold back on offering opportunities and benefits that will be of great importance to our life because they know we have the habit of leaving everything to the last minute.

Constantly postponing essential tasks and delaying action can make people believe we are unreliable. When we keep promising to get something done and putting them off for another day there is a tendency that we will lose the trust and respect of others. At some point, we will be view as an inconsistent person and a liar; there is also the risk of not fulfilling our life's ambition and loss of dignity. Overcoming procrastination requires a change in perception about the task at hand. Instead of managing to avoid significant activities that have a profound impact on the trajectory of our happiness and life purpose by dedicating our time to smaller mundane tasks that are less fulfilling, we should focus more on what we think we can do better to overcome this self-inflicted habit.

❖ Poor Decision Making

Philosopher William James once wrote, *"Nothing is so fatiguing as the eternal hanging on of an unfulfilled goal."* We give different unnecessary excuses as to why we cannot complete tasks such as specific deadlines and this has the tendency to impact our decisions in relation to the tasks and every other activity. Everyone has strengths and weaknesses but focusing on what we're not good at or being afraid to experience the unknown makes us feel hesitant to really push ourselves outside our comfort zone.

Procrastination can rob us of control over situations and puts us in a position to make poor decisions under deadline pressure. When we procrastinate, and make decisions during the period we are making decisions based on criteria that most likely wouldn't be there if we were sticking to deadlines. Putting off task completion till the last minute can be very destructive and can cause other people to suffer from the impact of delay. Emotional influence resulting from the pressure of time can literally influence our decision making during procrastination period and our stress levels will increase to a state where we become afraid to make effective decisions. Poor decision making can have huge negative effect on our results and happiness. To help overcome this procrastination phenomenon our key prevention measures must include choosing a relationship that supports accountability and rebuilding decision-making skills.

The Difference is clear between Active and Passive Procrastination

There is no doubt that procrastination is a universal problem but it is still a curable disease. The more we procrastinate the worse we feel about it. To understand how to overcome this self-defeating behaviour that is undermining our power of productivity, we first need to know what we are dealing with. The two most common types of procrastination that exist in today's society are Active and Passive. Knowing the difference between these forms of procrastination will enable us to identify which category we fall into when we exhibit this harmful behaviour and how to fix it to increase our efficiency.

1. Active Procrastinator

An active procrastinator is person that delays activities because they need more time to plan. They are capable of acting on their decision in a timely manner but they deliberately choose to postpone important task completion because they have other tasks assigned to them at the same time. Active procrastinators don't avoid their tasks but they enjoy and prefer working under intense pressure. They are good at diverting their attention to the less difficult activities first and leaving the most important tasks till last minute. And because an active procrastinator is aware of the risk that he is subjecting himself to when working on a task that is closer to deadline he displays high levels of reliance and self-confidence. Apart from being intrinsically motivated, active procrastinators use more task-oriented coping strategies when working under pressure. The major difference between these two groups of procrastinators is that active procrastinators get the task done with a few other tasks along the way before deadline, while passive procrastinators put off the task, worried about it, and often end up not finishing the task at all.

2. Passive Procrastinator

Passive procrastinators are paralyzed by their inability to act when a task deadline is around the corner. They put off task completion because they get easily overwhelmed when the task is more than they can handle. This category of procrastinators has low self-esteem in completing tasks and once they can't meet a deadline they become depressed, fearful and stressed out. A passive procrastinator runs away from responsibility with the notion that if they are not the one making the decision the result won't be their fault. They doubt their ability to perform on certain tasks, which is the key reason why they put off a lot of things.

Passive procrastinators experience more negative affective consequences of their actions with regard to self-control. The situation of passive procrastinators often becomes worse when they are experiencing fear and they suffer from lack of assertiveness, which impacts their confidence and self-image. Procrastination is a habit that is detrimental to every aspect of our life but the good news is we can overcome it. Annihilating this self-destructive behaviour will make us super-efficient and enhance our ability to bring out the hidden potential that is right inside us waiting to be tapped into.

Bridging the Gap of Procrastination

The procrastination phenomenon will not only put us at the risk of emotional discomfort if it is not overpowered, it will also cause us to exact a steep toll on our finances and inadvertently sell out on our happiness. To get out of this deeply ingrained pattern of behaviour we must develop an unflagging commitment and discipline in our daily routine. We must prime ourselves to tackle each task as soon as it arises rather than letting them pile up over time. Doing something, no matter how small, will get us close to our set target. Zig Ziglar, a known scholar in the area of personal development, affirmed, *"You don't have to be great to start but you have to start to be great."* To put it simply, when we take on key activities as soon as they arise we will discover that these activities gradually become easier to accomplish and increase our confidence to overcome the other challenges of life that revolve round them. Here are some of the practical techniques that we can use to overcome procrastination once and for all.

❖ Prioritizing Activities

Prioritizing everything on your to-do list with an estimate of how long it will take is another viable way of defeating procrastination. Doing this on a regularly basis will enable you to easily identify key priorities to focus on and the ones to avoid for the time being. If you are prone to deliberately delaying the completion of key activities, organizing your activities into manageable chunks will help annihilate the habit of putting things off indefinitely or switching focus. After all, habits only stop being habits when we avoid practicing them. Organized people successfully get things done because they create effective schedules which enhance their ability to stay focused and meet their deadlines.

When a workload is broken down into realistic and doable steps with consideration for the level of importance of each task on the to-do list, one is less likely to be overwhelmed. It is important to understand that procrastination is not an unchangeable habit. Regardless of why we procrastinate, we can still block its influence over our ways of living if we master scheduling our activities in priorities.

❖ Set Deadlines

According to Harvey Mackay, *"Deadlines aren't bad. They help you organize your time. They help you set priorities. They make you get going when you might not feel like it."* A task without a deadline isn't a to-do but rather a want to-do. Setting deadlines is critical if we really want to overcome procrastination and achieve our goals in life. To make things happen in any area of our life we need to set realistic deadlines, which start with writing down the task that we want to accomplish and adding a specific timeline to its completion. When we create deadlines for ourselves, it forces us to think through steps that we need to achieve them. For a success driven individual a deadline is an engaging challenge that leads to an opportunity to generate value. Set deadlines help motivate us to tackle essential activities.

In the real sense of things, it enables us to quickly identify the key activities on of our priorities list that we need to focus on and prevents us from getting overwhelmed by the volume of tasks that lie before us on a daily basis. When we don't set activities with deadlines we don't have the tendency to push ourselves and that leaves us vulnerable to procrastination. Procrastination has a way of making opportunities slip through one's fingers when a deadline is not set for every task that one wants to actualize. It is vital that we set deadlines and work toward each activity based on the time we allocated to it. Doing this daily will not only help us reduce stress, anxiety, fear and limiting beliefs in our ability, it will also eliminate the power of procrastination over our daily decisions.

❖ Build Accountability

One of the most unique powers of accountability is that it put us in the state of responsibility for all our actions. When we are accountable to our partner, mentor or our community we often get things done. While we can be accountable to others easily, it is quite difficult to be answerable to ourselves when there is no one else monitoring and holding us responsible. An important way to achieve deadline in any activities or goals is to have someone hold us accountable for our actions. Choosing someone that will ask us key questions on the state of things with the activities or goals that we set for ourselves helps us to keep focused and determined. Becoming accountable is the cornerstone for every great achievement.

Accountability buddies hold us responsible for meeting deadlines, accomplishing goals and making progress. According John Lemme, *"Accountability separates the wishers in life from the action-takers that care enough about their future to account for their daily actions."* When we a build sense of accountability we tend to look beyond the immediate moment and consider the consequences of disappointing ourselves in the presence of ones that we respect the most. This gives us a higher chance of actually getting the most important things done and avoiding distractions.

Having an accountability buddy can be a source of inspiration, excitement and motivation because it enables your partner keep an eye on the ultimate results that you said you want to accomplish by supporting you in recommitting your oath to your dream. To trick ourselves into meeting self-set deadlines and eliminate the habit of procrastination we must have an accountability partner that will enable us to keep our commitment to our set objectives and goals.

❖ Reward Progress

Our behaviour is strongly driven by reward. When we get rewarded for a behaviour we will repeat that behaviour in the future. Rewarded behaviours get repeated and unrewarded behaviours die out. The power of rewarding ourselves after completing an essential task that is dear to our heart is one of the behavioural psychologies that can help eradicate our procrastination habit. Giving oneself credit for doing something right is the starting point of reward for progress achieved. Self-criticism that aligns with the belief that we haven't done enough and the harsh beating of ourselves up after we have completed certain major activities are sure-fire recipes for regret and procrastination.

Whatever the exact reason, procrastinators rarely give themselves credit for doing something right, which makes them miss out on building up a positive, healthy habit. Paradoxically, procrastinators are either feeling guilty about not working or see themselves as burdened because of their incomplete work. To overcome this misery of procrastination we must inculcate the habit of rewarding ourselves for every little progress we make on any of the deadlines we set for ourselves. Rewarding ourselves for hard work is highly essential if we want to dig ourselves out of procrastinating habits. To better endure the periods of boredom and discomfort in what we do, we need to regularly reward our accomplishment.

"A man who procrastinates in his choosing will inevitably have his choice made for him by circumstance."

-Hunter S. Thompson

QUICK REFLECTION

1. Procrastination is putting off things that we ought to do to enable us to move forward in any area of our life. Why is it important to overcome our procrastination habits?

2. Has your procrastination ever caused you to miss out on life's opportunities? What are three habits that you must master in order to neutralize your procrastination habits?

3. What are the two most common types of procrastination that exist in our society today?

4. Before reading this chapter, what came to your mind when you heard the word "procrastination"? List some of the obvious side effects of procrastination.

CHAPTER 5

ACTION DRIVE PURPOSE

"Do you want to know who you are? Don't ask. Act! Action will delineate and define you."

-Thomas Jefferson

Acting is a way of making things happen. The philosophy that revolves around acting has a lot to do with getting things done, taking steps and making a move toward our life's desire. This important element that enhances the creation of our heart's desire is rooted in effort. To see the light of the day in any area of our life, action must come into existence through effort. The art of acting is the beginning of putting reality in place with the assurance for our dreams to touch the world around us. Action leads to results. According to Pablo Picasso, the most dominant and influential artist of the first half of the twentieth century, *Action is the foundational key to all success.* Adopting an action-oriented life will make us more productive in any area of our life. Our ability to get things done determines our speed of advancement in life. The longer an idea sits in our head without an action to tap the potential that encompasses its uniqueness, the weaker the idea becomes. For us to actualize the greatness that revolves around our dream we need to master the art of taking consistent action. If we do nothing else but focus on getting things done through commitment we will turn our aspiration into reality and see it in existence.

Taking action is often easier said than done; that is why a lot of people succumb to procrastination. Some of you that have experienced the same scenario will understand what I mean by that. Even though we might have set up a well-designed plan, life is often unpredictable and unexpected circumstances can arise out of nowhere to prevent us from taking that calculated step that we have already set for ourselves. Having lots of to-do lists without taking steps toward any can be overwhelming and make you stressed out. Inaction can be demeaning and can affect our ability to bring out the best of who we truly are. These limiting obstacles to action can create anxiety, self-doubt and fear. But the reality of life still aligns with the fact that what we do defines who we are, what we will become and what we can accomplish. *Action motivates achievement.* Becoming a constant action taker requires an insane amount of dedication and timeless commitment. It is also an art of risk-taking that revolves around discipline.

The bigger our action toward our set target, the greater our level of achievement. Embracing the habit of acting is crucial to our long-term achievement in any endeavours because it contains that symbolic power to build self-confidence and eliminate the power of fear over our ability to create. The only thing more daunting than taking action is not taking action. Dale Carnegie, the famous developer of the course in self-improvement and author of How to Stop Worrying and Start Living, once said, *"Inaction breeds doubt and fear. Action breeds confidence and courage. If you want to conquer fear, do not sit home and think about it. Go out and get busy."*

Results come to those who "Keep Acting"

One unique virtue that put this media mogul at the top of the A list in the firm industry today is his unstoppable action. Emmitt Perry Jr.'s childhood was marked by poverty and a household scarred by abuse. For years, he suffered brutal physical abuse at the hands of his father and several sexual abuses at the hands of several adults inside and outside his home. Every day, he lived in fear that something would set his father off. It got so bad that he took the drastic measure of attempting to kill himself. Although his situation was totally frustrating and frightening, Perry would go places in his mind to overcome these tragic moments. At 16, Perry changed his first name to Tyler to separate himself from his father and the painful memories of the past. Trying to find his way professionally, he held a series of unfulfilling jobs but still Perry never stopped taking steps to overcome the struggle that life handed to him to change his destiny.

Disappointed yet determined, Perry discovered his true passion while watching an episode of Oprah Winfrey's talk show. Perry was so inspired by Oprah's comments about why it's cathartic to start writing down the difficult events that happen in our lives that he took action and started to write down the difficult life experiences that he had encountered. He started with a series of letters to himself and through these letters he came to terms with his childhood and even brought himself to the point where he was able to forgive his father. Perry kept taking action and he was able to come up with "I Know I've Been Changing" as a musical based on those letters he had been written in his journal to himself. Through it all, Perry kept acting and became so dedicated to his belief that he rented a theatre with all his savings of $12,000 to put on his show. Unfortunately, his gambling on life did not pay off and his musical failed horribly. After several unsuccessful shows, at 28 years of age the playwright was homeless and broke, but Perry was not ready to give up on himself. For six years Perry took on a slew of odd jobs while living on the street because he could not afford to pay rent.

Despite all his efforts, the play continued to do poorly. Perry was just starting to think about quitting the whole writing career when he decided to act one more time and stage one last show. This last action led to personal breakthrough; the play opened in the summer of 1998 at the House of Blues in Atlanta and sold out eight times in a row, and the rest is history. Today Tyler Perry is an American actor, comedian, filmmaker, writer and songwriter who has produced many stage plays and won many awards. When what you are working on is difficult and it seems there is no way out of it or all the roads are closed against you, my special advice to you would be to keep acting by taking one more step and the light will surely appear at the end of the tunnel of history if you don't quit. Tyler Perry's story comes with one lesson, and that is taking action is vital to our life transformation and achievement.

Whenever we decide to take action the pieces of the puzzle of our life start to fall in place and with each piece unfolding we begin to see more and more of the bigger picture with the ways to actualize the achievement. The key questions right now are what are the things we need to do in order to keep acting? **In the next paragraph,** I will share a few with you that may seem simple but make a massive difference once implemented

Embrace the Habit of taking action

Whether good or bad, positive or negative, change is one inevitable art that empowers action. As a creature of habit, getting things done through consistent action is the pivotal step to a life of unlimited achievement. People who take real action that was needed to create their set objectives and do not allow the circumstances of life to imprison them in their comfort zone tend to experience greatness. They see every challenge along their way as an opportunity to overcome their limitation and fear over what is possible for them. They foresee their own possibility and use their action to materialize it. We can condition ourselves to imbibe the culture of getting things done if we put these questions to ourselves every time we are stuck or have the intention to procrastinate.

- What is my main reason for completing the task?
- How will it make me feel when it's finally done?
- How will it improve my life?

Awareness of the causes and impact of any decision is the recipe for overcoming the limitation of such a decision. Until we take action toward our set objectives, we have no knowledge of our strength, ability and what is possible for us. The choice to take action or not will ultimately determine our results in life. If we want positive results we must master the habit of taking consistent action. In order for us to successfully implement this habit here are some of the steps that we must follow:

1. **Get Started** -To improve ourselves, our growth and our achievement in life, we need to have a doing mindset and the only way to make this happen is to get started.

The science of life dictates that to get from one stage of life to the other we need to take one step at a time. Lao Tzu's profound statement, *"The journey of a thousand miles begins with a single step."* affirms this philosophy. Just envisioning something without taking gradual steps to its completion will do us no good. In fact, it will only encourage possibility blindness, which will materialize into stress and frustration. We can never get real progress if we don't master the art of taking baby steps toward our set objective. The other addiction that we need to desist from is attempting to start all our list of activities at once. This attitude can lead us to the land of procrastination by making the task too overwhelming for us to cope with. Getting started is all about taking each phase of the task one step at a time until we get engrossed and passionate about its completion. So instead of imbibing the spirit of analysis paralysis and thinking that you have to learn or know everything before you start, I would persuade you to get started with a little and build your momentum along way.

"We don't need to be great to get started but we have to get started to be great."

-Zig Ziglar

2. **Get Out of Your Comfort Zone –** Simply quoted by Neale Donald Walsch, *"Life begins at the end of our comfort zone."* Living and acting outside of our comfort zone is by definition uncomfortable; that is why a lot of people want success but are not willing to endure the pain and pay the price that comes with it. Accomplishing any

goals that we set for ourselves requires massive action and unwavering commitment. For us to successfully take action toward the achievement of our success we must be willing to drive our desire to remain in our comfort zone into a corner and set ourselves free to act massively without any limitation to how far we are willing go in life or how much we are willing to pay in actualizing the reality of our belief. Becoming comfortable in a state of inaction can cost us our dream and leave us in the agony of poverty for a lifetime.

The only way out of this misery is to understand our fear and identify what exactly is holding us back in our comfort zone. Then keep taking disciplined action gradually to overcome our inability to act. There are bound to be challenges whenever we start something new but if we persist till the end, it will surely and slowly pay off. By getting into the habit of putting our decisions into action, we are in a better position to raise our standard and create unimaginable progress for ourselves. There is still one more step that you can take if you want to move your life to the next level, and that is to turn your comfort zone into your commitment arena for taking action.

3. **Avoid Perfectionism** – Perfectionism is an art of dishonoring one's ability by telling oneself that there are certain things that need to be in place or be achieved before one is good enough to do the tasks and activities that one has a strong desire to complete. Perfectionists have the tendency to set a standard that is so high that it becomes impossible for them to achieve because they nurture the belief that anything short of perfection is

horrible. This type of thinking is self-defeating and can prevent us from taking action toward the accomplishment of our set objectives. Many of us are guilty of this; when I wanted to start my YouTube channel, I was so engrossed with the philosophy that everything must be in place before I could shoot or record any video, that I must have the right camera, studio lighting, location and even stay in a particular position when doing the recording. This put me in a state of denial and I kept procrastinating until my mentor challenged that mentality with a deadline for me to either release my first video after that day's accountability session or stop being her mentee, then I forced myself of out the misery of perfectionism.

The amazing thing about life is that wonderful things happen when we stop worrying so much and start taking action. Success in anything, including overcoming our habit of perfectionism, is about action. Commit to creating something daily and your work in progress will at some point lead you to the actualization of your breakthrough. As Arthur Ashe once said, "Start where you are. Use what you have. Do what you can." Take one step at a time toward your vision and do not let your unnecessary standards that you set for yourself prevent you from creating your destiny. Perfection does not propel action but action brings our perfection.

"My dreams are worthless, my plans are dust, my goals are impossible. All are of no value unless they are followed by action. I will act now."

-Og Mandino

81

The Benefits of Taking Consistent Action

Action is the silver bullet that will open up the gate of success if it is consistently implemented. Taking action not only separates the dreamers from the doers, it also fills the action takers with confidence as they start to see their objectives being accomplished each day as they act on them. Taking action creates possibilities that did not exist before. It empowers and enhances our ability to overcome our inaction that emanates from our fear. It is only in the flow of action that our life becomes meaningful and our vision becomes clear and attainable. Taking consistent action carries the potential to bring imagination and reality together. Jane Austen affirmed, *"It isn't what we say or think that defines us, but what we do."* Here are some of the benefits that those who cross the threshold from being just a dreamer to an action taker enjoy for experimenting with their possibilities.

❖ **Dream Fulfillment**

> The path to the achievement of our dreams may not be rosy or easy but having that burning desire to take consistent action toward its fulfillment gives us a sense of purpose in life. Passionate achievers use action as a tool to materialize their dream. They adore taking necessary action because it points them in the right direction and keeps them engaged. Aside from that it gets them interested in something meaningful and gives them an experience that is worth sharing. Having a dream of who we want to become and working toward its fulfillment is an important part of being human. The more we are willing to take action toward the fulfillment of our dreams the more likely we will

achieve them, and achieving them will make us feel more successful and happy in life. Stirring into action equipped every great achiever with the ability to unlock their potential and use it to joyfully fulfill their ambitions. The most astonishing truth about taking action is that it shapes our behaviors and transforms our personality. Devoting as much time as we can into taking constant action will yield a fruitful result if we don't quit.

❖ **Growth and Knowledge improvement**

In the process of taking action learning takes place and the action stimulates growth, which ignites knowledge acquisition. Tony Robbins, the guru of personal development, was on point when he affirmed that *"knowledge is potential; action is the power."* Action transforms our potential into achievable opportunities that create growth. Top achievers know that daily action opens doors to new ideas and new ways of creating solutions to world problems. Committing oneself to a sustained effort over a long period of time leads to mastery, which enhances confidence building and knowledge improvement. Taking consistent action is the key to continuous growth and goals achievement. Many people hinder their growth by refusing to take action, and this impacts their ability to grow physically and intellectually. Without a full commitment to action we are sabotaging our chance of fulfilling our dream. Unstoppable action gives us access to learning from our mistakes and correction to what we have been doing wrong. The difference between those who will become successful in actualizing their set goals and those that will not will be determined by the level of action they are willing to take each day toward their goals.

❖ **Overcome Fear and Excuses**

Taking unstoppable action is doing more than the average person would do under the same circumstances. Consistent action suppresses fear and gives one the courage to see beyond one's inability. Successful achievers are not fearless but master their fear and uses it to their own advantage. They train themselves to take action despite their fear. The uniqueness of becoming addicted to consistent action rituals is that limiting excuses become incapacitated and one explores the possibilities of opportunities that are not visible when one is inactive. Dreams become clearer and the innate desire to accomplish them is rekindled. Peter Nivio Zarlenga asserted that "action conquers fear." My question to you as you approach the end of this chapter is what kind of fear is holding you back from taking that step that will lead you to your breakthrough in life? As paradoxical as it may be, I want you to know that you will always experience fear and worry because that is the way we are wired but it is not the fear, it is what you do after the fear that determines who you become and where you will get to in life. *Kill your fear before your fear kills your dream by committing to doing at least one task every day.*

"Taking action! An inch of movement will bring you closer to your goals than a mile of intention."

-Dr Steve Maraboli

QUICK REFLECTION

1. After reading through this chapter what are the two things that you think it's important to keep in mind?

2. If we want positive results in any area of our life we must be consistent in our action. Why do you think this is necessary?

3. Identify two benefits of taking consistent action. List three ways that you will use the steps mentioned in the chapter to enhance your ability to take massive action on your plans.

4. Looking at your present situation, what do you think is holding you back from taking massive action and what are you going to do about it from now on?

CHAPTER 6

COMMITMENT
IGNITES REALITY

"Commitment creates consistency as action intensifies the fulfillment of our heart's desires. Be relentless."

-Ayo Jimmy

If there is one thing that will fast-track our movement toward the achievement of our goals and kindle our innate desire to visualize the reality of its existence before it materializes, it is uncompromised commitment, also known as undeterrable devotion, to do whatever it takes. Without commitment, our discipline is bound to waver because commitment is the mechanism that ignites the action which bridges the gap between goals and reality. The people that are committed use consistency as a tool to turn their challenges into chances to actualize their dreams. They outlast their obstacle by going extra mile and sticking to the existence of their possibilities. Marcia Wieder asserted, *"Commitment leads to action and action brings your dreams closer."* Concerning the acts of creativity and success actualization there is one elementary truth which defies the law of science and that is the moment one decides to commit wholeheartedly to the fulfillment of their beliefs, Mother Nature starts to execute her power of creativity to ensure that there are ways and methods of bringing that imaginary vision into fruition. All sorts of things occur to help one that would never otherwise have occurred. Heidi Reeder believed so much in this philosophy that she once said, *"Commitment is the foundation of great accomplishment."* Her statement affirmed that it is improbable we will reach greater heights if we fail to back our decisions up with uncompromised commitment.

Commitment equips us with the ability to shoulder responsibility for every one of our actions and conditions our mind to focus on what we need to do in order to bring our dreams to reality. The story of Bill Murray, a surviving prisoner of World War II, captured by the Germans, sheds more light on how unshakeable commitment toward our hearts desire can turn the hands of time in our favour. While in the German cell in Marisch Trubeau, a town near Czechoslovakia, Murray wrote the first draft of his book on mountaineering in Scotland on toilet paper donated by the Red Cross. His German captors the Gestapo, discovered the manuscript, confiscated it and destroyed it. To the amazement of his fellow prisoners, Murray's response to the loss was to start again despite the risk of being caught again and his physical condition which resulted a from near-starvation diet. With access to paper and a library he rewrote the book <u>The Feeling for Beauty Mountains Inspire</u>. It was this second version that became famous and inspired international interest in mountaineering.

Bill Murray's story shows that there is a great difference between being interested in achieving something and having the unshakeable commitment to do whatever it takes to achieve one's goals. The goal getters and great achievers of this world damn the consequences when they are on a mission to actualize their dream or fulfill their destiny. They risk their life as the expense of their purpose. Commitment brings clarity that empowers our decision to act. Where we are today is due to the level of commitment that we made toward the key decision in our life over the years. We have the power to transform our situation if we are willing to have unshakeable devotion to all our action.

The Special Deliverer

Here is another magnificent account that illustrates the importance of staying committed to your dreams. Tom Monaghan was four years-old when his father died and his mother felt incapable of caring for him and his brother while she attended nursing school. Tom and his younger brother James spent most of their life in foster homes and orphanages. When he was a freshman in high school, he decided that he wanted to be a priest but he could not endure the discipline of seminary. Due to that he was expelled for talking in the chapel and conducting a pillow-fighting. He returned to public school to try his chance in education. Monaghan graduated 44th in a class of 44. He wrote this statement under his photo in the 1955 class year book: "The harder I try to be good, the worse I get; but I may do something sensational yet." Monaghan's dream of studying architecture at the University of Michigan was jeopardized by his poor grades and lack of finances. He enlisted in the Marine Corps and by the end of his three years' tour, he had saved $2000 for tuition but he naively invested the money in a get-rich-quick scheme with an unscrupulous oilman; unfortunately for him, he lost his money and never saw the oilman again.

In 1990, Monaghan and his brother James borrowed $900 to purchase a small pizza store. Monaghan threw himself into the business, putting in upwards of 100 hours per week but his brother grew tired of the grind and when the business was losing so much money his brother opted out. Monaghan traded his Volkswagen for his brother's half of the business. Then he started to experience challenges. Fire burned his pizza shops down but the insurance company paid him no a penny on each dollar he lost. Although he was frustrated and discouraged he made the decision to commit his heart and soul to being a pizza man. He had a calling with a clear purpose and he was ready to do whatever it took for the future success of his business. During one of his business engagements the idea of stressing 30 minutes' delivery with menu simplification of sizes and toppings to give customers a quality pizza grew. This innovative idea kick-started the beginning of the first delivery services to customer's doorstep. Three years ago, Tom Monaghan sold 93% of the stock ownership of Domino Pizza to Bain Capital for an estimated $1billion. Due to his commitment, today there are over 13,811 Domino Pizza delivery locations around the world. I don't know what your dream is but one thing is for sure: if you stay committed to that dream of yours you will outgrow your adversity and create your achievement. *Stay committed to your dreams.*

The Benefit of Uncompromised Commitment

In today's world where commitment has become an option based on feelings we can decide to follow through with our decisions and do what we say we are going to do when we say we are going to do it. Mastering the act of commitment will open us to a lot of possibilities and successes. It will give us the opportunity to progress in life. To truly grow and expand we must find an area of our life where commitment supersedes comfort. Here are some of the benefits that you will enjoy for hanging on to uncompromised commitment.

1. Better Understanding of Yourself

When we are working toward our dream we are bound to experience different challenges in life and our commitment toward overcoming these stumbling blocks shapes who we are and guides us toward the perfect understanding of our abilities, weaknesses and strengths. Our level of commitment acts as the ammunition that foretells our adaptability and endurance capacity. It enlightens us as to our unlimited power to create the impossibility, and that is one of the reasons why we rekindle our energy to go the extra mile when we are ready to give up. Committed individuals are more likely to reach their goals and achieve success than those who take the easy way out.

Commitment connects us to our inner self and keeps us sharply focused. When we are constantly committing ourselves to the achievement of every activity that we set for ourselves as a target we will experience a deeper understanding of what makes us unique and capable of creating our own possibilities. If we want to be successful and happy in life we have to be committed to a task or activities that will give us a greater understanding of our true personality.

2. Better at Problem Solving

We cannot improve unless we consistently seek out and solve problems. Most problem-solving skills and abilities are developed through commitment to daily responsibilities. The act of committing oneself to daily challenging responsibilities unlocks the true potential of one's mastery of effective problem solving. Committed people see a better way of doing things because they engross themselves in consistent practice and do not give up when things are not going as planned. Uncompromised commitment opens their inner eye to see alternative ways around problems. It equips them with the daily habit that builds the possibility of creating the three Ss (system, structure and strategy) that lay the groundwork for unique problem solving tactics. *"Most people fail, not because of lack of desire, but because of lack of commitment"* as Vince Lombardi the legendary football coach put it. Before becoming an expert and a genius of all time Thomas Edison failed in creating the light bulb for 9,999 times but his uncompromised commitment provided him with better understanding of how to solve the mystery of the light bulb. Making a greater commitment to what we want to achieve will not only transform our belief of possibility, it will also create resilience and motivation to develop a strong desire for solving imaginable problems.

3. Better at Time Management

The commitment we exhibit toward our daily objective determines how we use and manage our time. Time management is a skill that takes time to master effectively and the power of its mastery lies in our level of commitment toward the achievement of our goals. According to William Penn, *"Time is what we want most but what we use worst."* When we are committed to the achievement of a task or an activity we passionately introduce the scheduling strategy of prioritizing each stage according to the time it will take to master the its achievement. The possibility of our achievement is embedded in what we commit ourselves and our time to.

Commitment enables us to focus on the importance of each activity and how to structure the time that we have judiciously to enhance its achievement. We all have 24 hours in a day and this will still continue into the foreseeable future. The key to better time management is to engross our daily hours, seconds and minutes into working on what we value the most in life and monitor how much time we commit to it. When you are totally committed to what you are most passionate about the time fly by quickly. Personal commitment is extremely important if we want to effectively utilize our time in turning our daily objectives to success.

"Commitment separates those who live their dreams from those who live their lives regretting the opportunities they have squandered."

-Bill Russell

QUICK REFLECTION

1. Reflect deep into your life and state three reasons why you have been unable to commit yourself to your set goals.

2. In your own words describe what commitment means to you and why you must commit yourself to the reality of your vision.

3. In what way to you think uncompromised commitment will be beneficial to your life transformation?

4. If there is anything to take way from Tom Monaghan's success story in this chapter what would that be?

CHAPTER 7

MIRRORING YOUR MENTOR

"Tell me and I forget, teach me and I may remember, involve me and I learn."

-Benjamin Franklin

To be the best it is quite essential to learn from the best. One unique thing about mentoring is that mentors help us to expand our perspective and shape our potential in ways that we simply can't do on our own. According to Oprah Winfrey, *"A mentor is someone who allows you to see the hope inside yourself."* Mentoring is one of the fast ways to transform the reality of our dream into fulfillment through the help of someone who has experienced life adversity and has the formula that will fast-track our journey to fulfillment. A mentor in simplistic terms is someone who has been there, experienced it and done that. They are the trusted advisers and role models that offer suggestions and knowledge of life experience to their mentees to help shape their decisions and destiny. Studies over the years have shown that most people who succeed have mentors; Having someone mentoring you through the journey of life is not a sign of weakness, it shows that you are smart enough to realize that success is not a one-man battle and are driven enough to succeed. Mentors see potential that we don't see in ourselves. Facebook icon Mark Zuckerberg was mentored by Steve Jobs, Google geniuses Sergey Brin and Larry Page mentored by Eric Schmidt and Oprah Winfrey was mentored by Maya Angelou. It is quite intriguing that there is a link between the most influential people's success and their strong mentoring relationship.

This denotes that if we want to experience unlimited success in any capacity, we owe it to ourselves to find a mentor or mentors. According to Sage Survey, out of over 1200 business leaders interviewed; 88% admit that mentoring helped them with the creation of successful businesses. A mentor teaches his mentees unique ways of doing things that will bring about changes and increases in ability and efficiency. Shawn Hitchcock once said, *"A mentor empowers a person to see a possible future, and believe it can be obtained."* A good mentor inspires, stretches, connects and opens the mind of his mentees to greater possibilities of what they can achieve with their unlimited potential. Mentoring provides us with the opportunities of tapping into the wisdom of those who have fought life in its territory and won. A mentor owns a wealth of experience that they can share with us that will help our hands to win as we journey through the struggle for greatness. When Richard Branson started Virgin Atlantic at over 40 years' age, he had one unique ability that kept him ahead of his competitor. He was willing to approach someone who was already running a business in the industry he was hoping to enter and asked him if he'd be willing to spare some time to give him advice on the challenges and successes of the industry. This quality earned Richard Branson a strong mentoring relationship with Sir Freddie Laker, whom he called on for advice because of his wealth of experiences with his own airline when he was launching Virgin Atlantic.

Having received help from business mentors Richard Branson's statement, "It doesn't matter if you are talking with someone who survived the start-up race or with someone whose business is coming crashing down. Learning from others mistake can be even more valuable," attests to the value that a mentoring relationship has in the success and achievement of mentees. As Zig Ziglar, an American author and one of the greatest businessmen of all time once said, "*A lot of people have gone further than they thought they could because someone else thought they could.*" Mentoring is the missing link between our action and the accountability for the successful fulfillment of our decisions. If we imbibe this mentality and have a board of advisors in different areas of our life, it will give us the advantage of being more nurtured toward the actualization of our dreams.

Standing on the Shoulder of Giants

Mentoring is one of the secret keys to abundant life and greater success. It exposes the mentees to constant advice from the best in their area of expertise. Apart from that, it gives them a shoulder to lean on in times of adversity. Anthony Robbins is a common household name where the subjects of personal development, success and high performance motivation are concerned. To his credit, Anthony Robbins has served as an advisor to leaders around the world for more than 38 years and empowered more than 50 million people from over 100 countries through his training program, audio and video. Tony, who worked as a part-time janitor at the age of 17, paid

$35 to attend a three-hour seminar by Jim Rohn the business philosopher whose indelible wisdom and success philosophy inspired Tony so much that he ended up working for him as a promoter of his seminar. Tony met Jim Rohn when the inspirational icon, who instilled in him the power of focus and the ability to master the control of his mindset, about 50 years ago. Tony learnt the legend taught that happiness and success in life are not the result of what we have; rather, how we live and what we do with the things we have makes the biggest difference in the quality of our life.

Jim Rohn's teaching influenced Tony's career and his ability to create a new vision for his own life, which empowered him to touch the lives of millions and millions of people. Mentorship gives the greatest and the most successful people the ability to learn how to win, no matter what happens to them in life. An achievement-oriented individual knows that there is a greater lesson to learn from someone who has journeyed through the path that they are planning to embark on. As a result, they look for counsel and advice that will help fast-track their processes and lift their hands as they win the game of life from the mentors, be it the header in their community, a business guru or master in his act.

The power of mentorship will enhance our ability to create the happiness that we desire and make our dreams come true if we know how to use it to our own advantage. Maya Angelou's advice to Oprah Winfrey changed her life and set her free from being weighed down by her past. What is it that is holding you down from chasing the reality, the future you believe in? Seeking the help of a mentor in that area of expertise can help re-shape your perception about the actualization of your true vision. Anthony Robbins' mentoring experience indicates a piece of advice or guidance from one's mentor can turn your dreams and the beliefs about the possibility of your future into an achievable reality.

Observation Mentoring

One of the unique ways that we can be effectively mentored is through the observation of the lives and successes of people that have gone through the path that we choose in lives. Studying the life of the greats and their successful achievement through reading their biographies and books will not only expose us to greater information and knowledge that we can model to shape and structure our dreams, it will also show us a clear picture that will enhance our certainty of the pathway to our future destination.

Observation mentoring is the blue print that gives the mentees sui generis opportunities to examine and learn different strategies and techniques that will fast-track their journey to great achievement. It acts as the lamp that lights their path to the unknown and gives them the courage to forge ahead with the belief that all they foresee and dream about the future is possible because they have seen people who have achieved the unimaginable. Isaac Newton attested to the reality of this philosophy with his statement, *"If have seen further than others, it is by standing upon the shoulders of the giants."* Reading through books on the life experiences and of stories on how the go-getters and the unstoppable achievers of this world overcame their struggles and conquered their adversities has a way of igniting within us to create our possibilities. It gives us that ability to see beyond our limitations and overcome every barrier that could have been a block to our life transformation and happiness.

Mentoring by observation is an empowering mechanism that has the power to equip the mentees with the intellectual ability to brain pick the knowledge and wisdom that successful people have been applying to solving problems that prevent a lot of people from navigating their course to abundant lives. It provides the mentees who research and study the life of the people they look up to with ability to know their true purpose and work tirelessly toward its fulfillment.

With mentoring by observation, we have the opportunity to create ourselves by mirroring the habits of great achievers. Confucius, the Chinese greatest philosopher, affirmed this theory with his saying, " *We hear and we forget. We see and we remember. We do and we understand.*" Brian Tracy, one of the greatest motivational public speakers and business gurus, adopted this philosophy and used the classic literature of success written by iconoclasts such as Napoleon Hill, Claude Bristol and Orison Swett Marden to kick-start his life transformation journey when he was 24 years old. Today Brian is not only the author of over seventy books that have helped people and businesses achieve their goals faster and easier than they can ever imagine, he has consulted for more than 1,000 companies and touched the lives of over 5,000,000 people across the globe.

The moral of this intriguing story is that, recorded history and biographies of people fulfilling their mission in life can be used to mentor ourselves to our future when we can have such people within our environment. Whatever your life goal is, find the list of books written by experts in that field and enlighten yourselves with biographies of the best in that area of expertise. Always remember that there is great power in using the lives of the great to sharpen ours by reading about what took them fifteen to twenty years of their lives to achieve and using their road map to shorten our journey to greatness.

The Benefits of Mentoring

In life, we all know that due to our imperfections we need help and support that will enable us to see challenges as opportunities to bring out our true potential. Asking for help and support of mentors and people that have experienced life and its games of adversity opens us to strength as we take the power of weakness away from our commitment to greatness. Mentors are confidantes who believe in the possibility of our vision and our ability to actualize it. They show this by offering us their unstinting support.

Aside from helping us to be ourselves, mentors' life experiences empower them with the ability to see a clearer picture of what we may not have comprehended or missed when planning our actions toward the path we choose in life. A good mentor will break us out of our comfort zone syndrome, encourage us to push boundaries and gain knowledge that will enable us to thrive in unknown territories. Why not approach someone whom you already know, be it in personal development or business, that has achieved spectacular things that you are aspiring to achieve today? Here are some of the reasons why mentoring is vital to success.

1. **Provides Impartial Advice and Encouragement**

    Putting oneself in the shoes of mentees is one of the key aspects of effective mentoring relationships. Great mentors enhance mentees' personal strengths through encouragement and constant motivation. They draw out the positive side of their mentees' vision by offering situation-specific advice and help to develop activities that will lead to the achievement of this life-changing process. Their impartial advice on situations and circumstances that might have been overlooked or ignored when life overwhelmed with competing priorities helps the mentees to gain clarity and commitment toward their life transformation. By sharing experience with mentees, they open their minds to possibilities and enrich their understanding that nothing in life comes easy as well as giving them the permission to learn from their own experiences.

Counselling from mentors helps great achievers move on and supports them in their career aspirations. Les Brown, one of the greatest motivational speakers understood the power of mentoring when he said, *"We ask for help not because we are weak but because we want to remain strong."* Study after study has found that people who get support and advice from mentors in areas where they are struggling display commitment toward the completion of activities that they set their minds to achieve. Mentors' actionable advice and encouragement can assist the mentees to discover their true potential and strength in their weaknesses without having to spend years of trial and error to find out for themselves.

2. **Expose You to New Ideas and Ways of Thinking**

Great opportunity for growth through exposure to new ideas that will broaden and challenge one's thinking is another benefit that the mentoring relationship creates for mentees. Mentors can be a great sounding board for new ideas and ways of thinking that can help mentees in overcoming hurdles and finding solutions to obstacles that are impacting their progress. Taking on new responsibility, be it in the area of business or career development, can be a bit challenging but with the support of a mentor that can point one in the right direction the process of achieving this objective can become easier.

This symbiotic relationship equips the mentees with the ability to learn that there is more than one way of doing things and that the issue of right or wrong is a matter of the mindset. Aside from ensuring that the mentees experience a continuous process of development, self-confidence and feedback, partnering with mentors will help the mentees get the best out of their potentials. Marion Lowrence, the owner of PA Hub, confirmed this with her statement, *"You may not realize your own potential but if someone else who can see your capability thinks you can achieve it, you feel more able to accomplish your goals."* Mentoring is a method of teaching and learning that enhances strategic thinking and definition of outcomes which, when achieved, can accelerate one's career and personal development.

3. Assist You with Problem Solving

One of the 'get me out of adversity and problems' cards offered by mentors is the solution strategy that helps mentees identify the major problems that they are experiencing and how to effectively address them. They ask questions that will allow their mentees to access their own internal wisdom. Mentors use their life experiences and the challenges that they have overcome as a lesson to preempt the needs of their mentees and advise them with consistence guidance on strategies and techniques that can be applied to solve the problem at hand. They encourage the understanding of the problems by listening, not being judgmental and providing insight that will help the mentees to discover the root cause of their own predicament. Mentors offer suggestions and knowledge that will enable their mentees to engage in logical reasoning that will lead to the development and capacity to identify major solutions to their problems.

As a role model, mentors have been there and done that; sharing their stories often presents a reassurance and different view to the possibility of the issue under discussion. In order to provide the mentees with their expectations and enable them to gain focus, mentors assess mentee's strengths and weaknesses and decide together with them on the best road map to use in overcoming that particular problem.

4. **Provide You with Opportunity to Develop New Knowledge and Skills**

Mentoring assists people in uncovering where they are in their career, where they want to go, what skills they need to develop and teaches them how to acquire the necessary knowledge and skills. Mentors inspire mentees to charge for the accomplishment of their goals and develop skills they never thought they were capable of achieving. They help them to think clearly and take

103

calculated actions that will result in the fulfillment of their dreams. Mentors advise on successful career navigation and foster positive thinking by helping the mentees to understand behaviors and mindsets that can detract them from their career development.

As result of their previous experience mentors see the blind spots that we do not see and act as a catalyst facilitator to help us shape our dedication to develop strategic skills and business successes. They connect us with networks of people that will enable us to tap into our full potential and use their influence to create long-term career and business progression. Mentors also illuminate a path and prepare the mentees to use positive thinking to empower themselves for the achievement of goals. Partnering with a mentor will not only equip you with knowledge and skills that will enable you to create a long-lasting achievement in life but will put you in a better position to contribute to the growth and future development of others as they advance toward their life transformation. Mentoring relationships can be rewarding and help us become accountable for our actions. They can increase our motivation and inspire us to develop personal qualities that will rekindle our greatness.

How to Find and Keep a Mentor

A guiding hand and some words of wisdom from a mentor go a long way to inspire positive imagination and action; that is why mentoring is one of the biggest keys to success. Partnering with a mentor is a vital tool for personal development because it helps shape the discovery of the mentee's true personality.

This relationship offers the mentee an opportunity to be invested in by someone who believes in the reality and achievement of his mission in life. For me, mentoring has helped me to have a successful journey through my life transition and equipped me with the ability to use my mind to create active possibilities in business and life style. If you want to achieve more of your goals and make a significant impact in the lives of others, here are some of the tips that I would like to share with you that have helped me in seeking out mentors.

- Identify a potential mentor to emulate
- Study the person and read biographies of great people whose life-style cum achievement I want to emulate
- Invite them out for coffee and ask them a series of questions
- Follow up with them after the meet-up to show that you are committed
- Stay committed to the relationship and processes and be eager to study
- Don't check out when you feel challenged
- Reciprocate (Give Back)
- Seek out more than one mentor

I do hope these tips will be of great assistance to you as they worked for me. Seek out a mentor and make the unimaginable happen.

"A mentor is someone who sees more talent and ability within you than you see in yourself and helps bring it out of you."

-Bob Proctor

105

QUICK REFLECTION

1. To be the best it is quite essential to learn from the best. After reading through this chapter do you think that statement is true? What are three important goals in your life that having a mentor will help you achieve?

2. Mentoring is a unique weapon that can enhance our ability to open the doors to great potential that lies untapped inside us. In your own opinion, what are the benefits you gain from being mentored?

3. List three opportunities that observation mentoring can open you to.

4. In what way is a mentoring relationship important to you? What are three ways you can use to find yourself a mentor?

CHAPTER 8

DISCIPLINE IS THE MAGIC POWER

"Discipline is the heart of diligence. Action is the power that propels it."

-Ayo Jimmy

Understand that this chapter is the most important part of this book. Without a proper mastery of this virtue, the rest will not do much for you. My suggestion to you is to read through this chapter as many times as possible. We all dream of bigger and better things, yet few people actually rise up and accomplish them. Why is that so? The truth to that statement is that the few who actually accomplish their dreams succumb to self-discipline and make consistent practice their best friend. Mike Tyson, one of the greatest professional boxers, summarized it with his saying, *"Discipline is doing what you hate to do, but nonetheless doing it like you love it."* Discipline is all about sacrifice; that is why Oxford Dictionary defines discipline as a way of life aimed at self-control and conformity. It is the lifeblood of achievement that is governed by diligence. In its simplest form discipline is having the ability to do what you need to do; even when you really don't want to do it.

Discipline plays a prominent role in every great achiever's success and life transformation. The act of discipline separates the men from the boys in the arena of life and empowers those who are diligent with the ability to replace unproductive habits with a practice that is highly productive. Bob Proctor, first mentor to Ray Stanford, attests to the power of discipline during his first critical conversation with his mentee, not because it is a nice to have attribute but because it is a highly essential virtue for successful achievement. Discipline can change our life if we are ready to embrace it and use it to produce opportunities that will generate results. If one is disciplined and has the willingness to pay the price for whatever he wanted to achieve in life, he will always get a positive result.

The life of Michael Jordan, one of the greatest basketball players to ever walk the earth, says it all about the impact of self-discipline on unstoppable achievement. Jordan was widely admired by his fans and his team mates for his self-discipline and limitless determination to push himself beyond his limits when practicing for his games. Each failure drove him to continuously master his skills and improve so as to prove to everyone that he was the best at what he did. Having the foresight to recognize what self-discipline aligned with consistent eight hour practices would do for his skills, Jordan was able to design practicing tactics that put him at the top of his ledge in every one of his games and that formed into a habit which reflected on his performance through his whole career. Discipline empowers with the ability to give ourselves command and be laborious enough to follow it through. We will never know what we can achieve unless we set a goal and go all out for it. The intriguing story of Jordan shows that a great commitment to self-discipline can lead to successful achievement. Self-made millionaires, scientists, inventors and sports legends have imbedded this philosophy and it works beyond reasonable doubt for them. Thomas A. Edison, the light bulb prophet, was a graduate of the school of self-discipline and mastered his act through this principle.

You may not have all that it takes to create that business or master that career but if you emulate the great by injecting self-discipline into your daily routine you will surely materialize the achievement of your dream. Being dyslexic, the writing of this book took me almost two years of my life but I imbedded the culture of self-discipline and committed certain hours of my time daily to do just a little bit of it; now the rest is history. If you take this principle to heart you can achieve whatever you set your mind on. Don't give up on yourself!

Engaging with Destiny

"*Self-discipline is an act of cultivation that requires you to connect today's actions to tomorrow's results. There's a season for sowing and a season for reaping; self-discipline helps you know which is which.*" This wisely profound statement by Gary Ryan Blair, the president of Goalsguy and author of **Goal Setting 101,** summarizes the importance of discipline in unstoppable achievement. Without any doubt, I agree with Gary that self-discipline is the hall mark of every great achievement. It grants its possessor self-command and the power to resist temptations and distractions that tend to stand in the way of greatness. Successful people make self-discipline habitual by doing things that they know they should do whether they like it or not, because they know that's one of the biggest prices they need to pay for the attainment of success.

As a matter of fact, discipline is something we can all develop. The more we practice it the better we become. George

Pehlivanian's intimate relationship with self-discipline began as a result of his sincere love for piano and violin at the age of three. As a kid Pehlivanian sacrificed the luxury of playing with friends and competing in sports for his love for piano and violin. He stays in his room and practiced for hours, mastering his craft and empowering his ability to become the best of the best in his field. In 1975 Pehlivanian and his family emigrated to Los Angeles where he went to study conducting with Pierre Boulez and Ferdinand Leitner. He spent two summers at the Academia Musicale Chigiana Siena, where he was awarded the Diploma di Merito. At age 25, Pehlivanian's self-discipline and consistent practice made Lorin Maazel notice his skills and talent when he was selected as the best out of the five students picked to conduct in front of Maazel at an American Symphony Orchestra League. This changed his life and since then Maestro Pehlivanian has conducted at many of the leading opera companies of both Europe and the United States. In 1991, he was awarded the Grand Prize at the Besancon conducting competition as the first American ever to receive this award. On the concert platform Pehlivanian has led many of the world's leading orchestras, including the London Philharmonic Orchestra. In winter of 2017 Maestro Pehlivanian made history as the first conductor of American descent to conduct a Turkish Orchestra, leading performances with the President's Symphony Orchestra of Ankara. Maestro Pehlivanian's intriguing story seals the fact that without discipline, success is a delusion for those wish for its achievement.

The sacrifice of the character in relation to self-discipline not only paid off but also made him a legend that will forever be remembered in operas and Orchestras. That desire of yours that you cherish so much can be achieved if you are willing to imbibe self-discipline in everything you do. I will end this paragraph with the words of Erma Bombeck that I kept like gold in the safest part of my heart because it's worth the value. *"When I stand before God at the end of my life, I would hope that I would not have a single bit of talent left and could say I used everything you gave me."* My question to you is will you? Don't let lack of self-discipline prevent you from having the confidence to say this.

The Benefits of Discipline

No personal success or goal can be realized without discipline. Discipline is the most important attribute needed to achieve outstanding performance and excellence in any activity. The virtuosity of success, apart from leaving clues, is that it requires a greater amount of hard work and self-discipline, which is the bedrock upon which this principle lies. Anyone running after a cause that is greater than them will agree with me that it can be a tough and lonely experience but discipline gives us the power to hang in there and follow things through; that is why it is a must-have ingredient for achieving goals. The possession of this skill will enable us to manifest the inner strength that will enhance our ability to persevere during tough times.

Self-discipline puts us in a position to reject instant gratification and pleasure in favour of greater gains that demand our limitless effort and focus for its achievement. On the other hand, lack of discipline can lead to a life of failure and disappointment. As the crucial pillar of real and stable success, discipline is needed at all times. Here are some of the benefits of discipline that can motivate you to master the act in whatever you do.

⚜ Discipline Paves Way for Success

Discipline brings self-control and clarity of thought, which is an enabler of positivism and self-inspiration. It improves our capability to make healthy decisions and follow them through without changing our mind. Self-discipline brings rules and regulations in our life. We make right decisions when we follow certain regulations and this puts us in a position to become more responsible, effectively manage our time and be accountable for all our actions. When we instill these traits, and begin to exhibit them, we start to get motivated to see through what we started, and this pave the way for us to succeed in our lives. Being disciplined does not mean living a limited lifestyle, nor does it mean giving up everything you enjoy. All it requires from us is the ability to learn how to focus our mind and maintain long-term perseverance until we accomplish success in what we set our minds on. Scheduling tasks on paper can help us focus our mind on strategies that we can implement to achieve set priorities. I express the power that lies behind the philosophy of recording your vision on paper in **Chapter 1.** Please take some time to reflect on *"Recording your vision on paper"* because it will put you in a better position to hold the keys that open the door to unimaginable success that is known to few. In the short term, discipline allows us to reach our goals in a reasonable time frame and live a more satisfying life.

⚜ Discipline enable us to Apt Satisfaction toward Life

If we are to be masters of our own destiny we must develop self-discipline. Discipline is necessary in all spheres of life. In fact, life is best enjoyed only when discipline is maintained. When self-discipline is implemented toward the achievement of a set objective it gives us hope, which creates an inner joy that metamorphoses into progress, and consistent progress leads to satisfaction and happiness. As Tony Robbins insightfully said *"Progress equals happiness."* Our ambitions and dreams will not only be achieved through living a life that is cultured by discipline; we will also experience a massive sense of satisfaction as we overcome each challenge that we encounter during this process.

Besides that, discipline gives us the power to face any hurdles and rise above them. With discipline, an average person can rise as far and as fast as his talents and intelligence can take him but without discipline the person with every opportunity and knowledge will seldom rise above mediocrity. If we want to succeed in anything in life, discipline is needed at all times. Aside from helping us to use our common sense and intelligence in new ways to create a satisfactory and happier life for ourselves, discipline inculcates in us the virtues of honesty and a sense of accountability.

⚜ Discipline Empower us to Build Inner Strength and Control Over Thoughts

Discipline enables us to create the inner strength that controls our mind, builds our character and helps us to overcome our weakness. As wisely stated by Napoleon Hill, "Discipline is very important, as it helps to keep our thoughts balanced and controls our action."

Whatever we engage in, whether it involves mental decisions or physical acts, self-discipline is needed to keep our emotions under control. If we lose the ability to maintain self-discipline when dealing with life challenges our emotions usually take over. The major problem with that is our reason for setting that objective or goals will fly out of the window and our decision will not likely be as productive as we expect it to be.

Discipline not only imbues us with the ability to control our actions and thoughts, it also bestows on us a strong feeling of enthusiasm. This is so because when we know our worth we start to accept ourselves and everything starts to change around us, and then the true version of who we are comes into the limelight. The clarity that discipline brings to our thinking improves our capacity to make viable and innovative decisions that allow a right balance between actions and the actualization of the objectives. Becoming habitual to self-discipline will instill the willpower that will ignite positive behaviour and strengthen our mental and moral courage.

Discipline will make You Unstoppable

The more disciplined we become the easier life gets. Discipline brings stability and structure into our life. Staying disciplined helps get things done faster and that leads to peace of mind. The ultimate end of imbibing self- discipline is that it makes you develop self-confidence and a burning desire that propels you to charge through adversity in order to accomplish remarkable achievements. No matter how grand our goals are, we will never taste victory if we are not willing to discipline ourselves and build momentum through hard work. True achievement is incubated in uncompromising decisions matched with consistent discipline and the right mindset.

Discipline allows us to choose from different options and by following these options through we can garner the success that we always sought. It takes discipline to master oneself and continue to show up even when you can't see the light at the end of the tunnel. Discipline puts us in the driving seat by keeping us focused on our purpose and the possibility of achieving it. We become insistent and proceed no matter what the circumstance may be. And as a result of our desire to make a difference we become unstoppable. In a nutshell, hard work aligned with self-discipline will lead to unstoppable action that will enhance great successes.

Mastering Discipline

The recipe for successful achievement of our plans and goals in life is to become more disciplined as an individual. Self-discipline is one of the most crucial factors for success and a happy life. Too often people either try to pretend their vulnerability don't exist or they try to cover it up, but having the confidence to own it puts us in charge and increases our possibility of overcoming that habit. To master the art of self-discipline we must be conscious of our weaknesses and continuously devote ourselves to purposes and techniques that will enable us to overcome those limiting habits. Self-discipline will give us the ability to take action irrespective of our emotional condition.

One of the things that makes self-discipline a sexy virtue to master is that it surpasses the power of mental toughness. Being a highly talented athlete is not a ticket to winning; if a highly talented athlete does not practice his skills regularly and master the art of discipline he will struggle physically during competition. This denotes that mental toughness without self-discipline is recipe for disaster. People with a higher degree of self-discipline do not allow impulses to dictate their choices. Instead they make levelheaded decisions that results in high performance with great achievement. If we are looking to take control of our choices and habits, here are some of the ways to help ourselves become more disciplined.

1. **Set Clear and Achievable Goals -** A realistic goal with a clear plan will put us in a position to set milestones and outline steps that will enable us to reach our goals on time. Higher achievers use these techniques to stay on track and establish their finish line. The clarity of mission and why it is important propel self-discipline. If we want to achieve our goals in life, we must discipline ourselves to repeatedly practice this process of setting daily goals with clarity and creating steps to follow them through. To avoid feeling intimidated, it is essential that we keep things simple and break our goals into smaller doable steps instead of trying to achieve them all in one go. Truth be told, the bigger your goals the more challenges one will experience to bring them to fruition, so hard work with immeasurable persistent is required. Self-discipline will act as the mantra that will keep us focused and committed toward the fulfillment of our heart's desire if we inculcate the habit. One other thing that can keep our discipline in check and help us monitor our

progress is to be aware of the actions that we take daily that help to reinforce our newly developed habits and make adjustments where needed.

2. **Take Small Steps** - The habits that we form daily strengthen or weaken our self-discipline. The problem with most of us is that we create habits that set us up for failure. We give up on things at every opportunity. Without discipline, nothing ever happens and nothing will ever change. Self-disciplined people know this secret; that is why they take incremental steps to liberate themselves from procrastination and indecision. The key fact is that we can desire, plan, decide and think positively but if we do not take action with immeasurable discipline we will still fall behind and lose control.

Disciplined people are the only ones who succeed because they start small and increase their steps along the way as they progress. They use the start small strategy to gain momentum. Mastering the art of self-discipline enhances the confidence of an achiever to take small steps toward the fulfillment of his heart's desire. Self-discipline drives action that creates micro changes and self-reliance. It enables the disciplined to see that there is an inherent good in doing things little by little. No matter what we are aspiring for if we start by taking one step at a time by daily disciplining ourselves to do it the activities it will become an enjoyable task that will later on metamorphose into success. And more importantly, we will overcome our fear of starting in the first place and be strong enough to face next life's challenges.

3. **Remove Temptation** - Mastering discipline becomes easier when temptation is removed. The removal of distraction and temptation that can impact our ability to stay focused on our life time objectives can help greatly in building our self-discipline. The choices and decisions of people with self-discipline are not dictated by their feelings and emotions. They spend less time deliberating on whether to indulge in behaviour that is detrimental to their health because they have self-control that enables them to weed out temptation. It only takes one moment of weakness to fall a victim of temptation and if it is not properly checked out through self-control it will result in a life time habit. Exercising self-control during temptation can enhance our ability to keep disruptive emotions and stressful circumstances under control. The fewer the distractions and temptations we experience, the more focused we will be in accomplishing our goals. Boosting our self-control is pivotal to the limitation of distraction and temptation. Despite what many people may think, engaging in daily meditation will help improve our self-control and enable us to have a disciplined life style.

4. **Fill Your Mind with Positive Information** – One of the hardest things people face is looking at things from the positive perspective. A lot of people struggle with this because we are wired naturally to think negative when things happen. Our ability to discipline the mind to think positively irrespective of what the situation before us reveals will empower us to create an unimaginable solution that will solve the problem at hand. Every bit of information that we feed our mind daily matters and

will determine how far we will go in life. The books we read, the programs we watch and the type of news we listen to are all programming our mind for either success or failure. As Zig Ziglar put it, "What you feed your mind determines your appetite." Nothing nourishes the mind with great thoughts like positive information. Feeding the mind with positive information can actually create value in your life and help you to become more disciplined.

Everything in our life will change automatically if we learn to inject positive information into our mind daily. Listening to fear mongering news and horrific stories will not take you to a good place in life. It will only ruin your dreams and future. Give positive energy to your mind by staying around people that will empower your ability to see things positively; this will amplify your greatness. Frank Outlaw expressed his own understanding of the impact of positive information on our thoughts and the way they can enhance our ability to create who we become when he wrote:

"Watch your thoughts, they become words; watch your words, they become actions; watch your actions they become habits; watch your habits, they become character; watch your character, for it becomes your destiny."

The power behind feeding our mind with positive information is immeasurable. When you fill up your mind with positivity and good information your life will not only change for good but it will shape your character and improve your self-discipline.

"Motivation gets you going, but discipline keeps you growing."
-John C. Maxwell

QUICK REFLECTION

1. Why do you need self-discipline to enhance your success actualization?

2. List three ways that self-discipline can help you overcome your weaknesses.

3. From the stories of higher achievers mentioned in this chapter, what are the two important things that you can take away and use to enhance the improvement of your self-discipline?

4. Identify some of the benefits that one will derive if one masters' acts of self-discipline.

CHAPTER 9

COURAGE IS THE HIDDEN SECRET

"Courage isn't having the strength to go on – it is going on when you don't have strength."

-Napoleon Bonaparte

Many of us are aware of who Walter Elias Disney is because of his animated cartoon character Mickey Mouse and Disney land but what we do not know about him is the secret behind his creativity. Walter was born into a family of five children and he grew up on a farm outside Marceline, Missouri. His passion for drawing was one thing that distinguished him from his siblings. From the age of four Walter started selling his drawings to neighbours to make extra money, as his family was poor and times were hard. At the age of nine Walter was getting up at 3:30am seven days a week to help his father fold and deliver newspapers for two hours before attending classes. His work responsibility did not keep him away from his love for drawing. In high school, Walter studied class work by day and went to art school at night. His courage kept him curious and active against all obstacles.

When he was 16 years old World War I broke out. Walter tried to enlist in the army but he was rejected. Against all odds and after a series of attempts that resulted in failures Walter found his passion in animation. He was courageous enough to drop out of high school to go into something he truly desired, 'animation'. Walter began making small animated cartoons for local businesses as a commercial artist. He opened his first animation studio only to file for bankruptcy one year later. This business eventually failed but Walter's fortitude to come back from failures with courage and enthusiasm never stopped. Walter began to look for other options. He packed his bags and moved to Hollywood, California where he and his brother Roy pooled their money, over two hundred and fifty dollars, together and borrowed over five hundred dollars more and started a business in their uncle's garage. Over the next few years, Walter and Roy worked on creating animated short movies and eventually they started hiring artists to work for them. Walter's courageous experimentation with a series of failures and consistent learning enhanced his creativity and in 1928 and Mickey Mouse was born. Walt Disney became famous for his American animation, the Walt Disney company and Disneyland. As Winston Churchill wisely said, *"Courage is going from failure to failure without losing enthusiasm."* It is the bedrock of every achievement. The heart of being courageous gives us the ability to chase the realization of our true identity without the fear of the unknown or the entertaining of naysayers' opinions of our possibilities.

Courage offers its apostles the power to make a difference and the ability to create the unimaginable. It aligns our confidence with action and consistency. Courage is acknowledging doubt that we have in our mind but pushing forward anyway. It is living a life that is driven by curiosity than fear. When starting anything in life there is always the uncertainty factor. These uncertainties often give rise to fear of failure, fear of loss, fear of rejection, the fear of looking foolish and the fear of being alone. Everyone is scared of one thing or the other; even our heroes that we viewed as the strongest at one time have been fearful, but the heart of courage differentiates them from others and makes them victorious over adversity. Courage is the secret sauce that encourages those who master it to put aside their fear of failure and jump by taking the first step. It is the power to see confidence in cowardice. As Nelson Mandela insightfully asserted, *"Courage is not the absence of fear but the triumph over it. The brave man is not he who does not feel afraid but he who conquers that fear."* Courage is the exceptional power in us that compels us to strangle fear of inaction. It empowers us to attempt things that we would not have tried. Sometimes, in the midst of struggle and life's challenges, we forget that we do have the power to be courageous each day of our lives but the truth of life is that we all have the capacity to be courageous.

The first step toward conquering any life challenge is to face it boldly and then use our innate drive as a motivator to overcome it. As David Viscott profoundly said, *"If we have the courage to begin, we have the courage to succeed."* Although not everything that we planned or envisioned will always happen as we expect it to but if we are resilient and keep working at it, we will surely have hundred percent success at the end. Courageous people stand up against things that threaten them and take action in a way that is consistent with their values. They follow up their beliefs with boldness and act on their convictions. Acting courageously will not only make you feel good and confident, it will also increase your state of happiness. Courage will give you the strength to evaluate your emotional response and act rationally toward the fulfillment of your dreams.

The Forgotten Hero that Held Courage for Ransom

The inspiring story of one of the exemplary people who felt fearful but acted anyway expresses in detail the importance of being courageous to achieve unlimited breakthrough. We become more courageous when we choose to confront the obstacles that life throws at our feet. According to Mark Twain, "Courage *is not the absence of fear; it is acting in spite of it.*" Glenn Cunningham was seven years old when he nearly died in an explosion that killed his brother Floyd. One cold morning Glenn and Floyd arrived at their one-room school and were slapped in the face by bitter cold wafting out of the still structure. Finding the class room empty and cold, the two boys loaded the large pot belly stove full of firewood and soaked the logs in lighter fluid for a bit. Floyd started the fire with a strike of a match, not knowing that the kerosene-labeled can in the room contained gasoline. Almost instantaneously, the fire took on a life of its own, exploded everywhere and engulfed Floyd in a horrific sheet of flame. Glenn was knocked to the ground by the mini-explosion and his legs were ravaged by the flames.

The doctor that attended to these two-brothers told their parents that Floyd was more dead than alive but Glenn would probably live unless infection set in; either way, Glenn would never walk again because his legs were burnt so badly that they became useless. After overhearing his pessimistic neighbour empathizing with his parents and advising they to face the reality of the fact that their only remaining son would never walk again, Glenn make a courageous decision to himself that he would walk again. Fortunately, his mother believed him when he tearfully told her this. Glenn resolved to walk again by dragging himself along the fence, stumbling as he tried to wheel his legs into function; no matter how much it hurt, he endured the excruciating routine as a necessary evil. Slowly, over a period of months, Glenn's legs began to heal and function. As Glenn began to walk again he made another discovery: his legs hurt like thunder when he walked but didn't hurt at all when he ran so for five to six years all he did was run everywhere. Before long, young Glenn was known throughout his community for his running. He never moved 10 feet without breaking into a run.

By the time, he was 12 years old, Glenn ran despite having legs that were still riddled with scars, and he outran everyone in his age group in high school. With no toes on his left foot and scarred legs Glenn set a national record, running a mile in 4 minutes, 24.7 seconds. Glenn later smashed the NCAA record in the mile, zipping to a time of 4:11.1, ran in 1932 Los Angeles, earned a berth on the U.S Olympic team and won a silver medal in the Berlin Olympics 1500-meter race. What exactly is it that you are aspiring for or you have dreamed about but the challenges of life are preventing you from take the step toward or making it look impossible to you? My prophetic advice for you is to summon the courage and take just a little step toward its actualization daily and the how to materialize it will reveal itself along the ways. I know it is quite easy to say just do this and that and thing will be fine, most especially if you are not the one experiencing struggle, but the truth of the matter is, you will encounter more challenges along the way before you witness greatness but always remember that these challenges are designed to shape your courage and character to create the reality of your heart's desire.

When people hear my story, particularly the part about me being dyslexic and writing books and also studying part time for my doctorate in innovation and strategic management, they will laugh and assert that it is impossible and some will even say to my face that I am setting unachievable goals for myself. I do not allow their opinion or pessimistic advice to imprison my courage because all they can see is the problems and not the purpose behind my actions. As Benjamin Disraeli once said, *"Nothing can resist the human will that will stake even its existence on its stated purpose."* Not only have I written three books, by the time you are reading this book I will have completed my doctorate, which seemed impossible to some but achievable to me. Are you ready to truly embody courage by honouring your heart like I did? You will only deny yourself the experience that your heart is longing for if you hesitate. Do not stall anymore, hoping for the right conditions; move forward now and you will be victorious.

The Need for Courage

Understanding exactly what we want is the foundation for our success. By necessity, our minds are designed to let fear in when we decide to engage in the creation of our belief but courage provides us with the ability to see fear as the impetus to grow stronger with high resilience. It is the willpower that enables a person to face difficulty with painful experience and still become bolder to create unbelievable results. Courage empowers us with the bravery to face circumstances that are impeding the exploration of our true potential and make drastic decisions with a follow-up of massive action. One of the major reasons courage is needed is to help us step out of our comfort zone and discover more about who we truly are. As Neale Donald Walsch asserts, *"Life begins at the end of our comfort zone."* Here are other reasons why cultivating the art of courage is essential.

🔸 To Turn Every Obstacle into an Asset

Our ability to summon the courage to go through life's challenges without the fear of failure will enable us to grow and see obstacles as an indispensable prerequisite and part of life's lessons for turning adversities into achievement. Any path we choose in life has its obstacles; that is so because nature uses adversities to test our true intention for what we say we real want and to get what we real desire we need to confront the obstacles with courage. Ryan Holiday mentioned Marcus Aurelius' profound saying in his book Obstacle is the Way: *"The impediment to action advances action. What stands in the way becomes the way."* We have the ability to turn obstacles into assets if we are willing to use them positively as tools that are meant to shape our intention to create our destiny.

The calmer and more confident we become when we experience challenges and adversity, the easier it will be for us to make decisions that will allow us to see the way out of these formidable obstacles. When we come from a place of centered calmness, courage is much easier to access and used as a weapon to empower our ability in turning every life's obstacle into an opportunity. We need courage to endure constant setbacks, disappointments and temporary defeats. If you experience challenges when chasing your dreams, you should always remember that opportunities are usually disguised as obstacles to help us on our path to greatness. If we endure and master each obstacle with calmness, it will surely lead us to our greatness. In simple words, the struggle we are facing is there to help us see a new perspective to growth and success.

⚜ To Persevere in the Face of Adversity

Within every adversity, there is an opportunity to improve our condition and create our destiny. We can become intimidated by adversity if we waste valuable time overanalyzing and questioning our ability to overcome it. Instead of thinking about our weakness we should focus our attention on the final outcome and embark on the activities that will lead us to its achievement by taking one step at a time. Knowing why we are doing something and how we want it to help define who we are is a vital anchor that will enable us to persevere when we face adversity. Life uses adversity as a trial to see if we will quit along the way but if we endure the suffering and persevere, we will gain momentum that will empower our innate desire to face life's adversity and courageously convert it into advantage for greatness.

Ordinary people shy away from adversity and give up too soon when things are not working as expected. What great people do is turn the pain of adversity into a plan for progressing with perseverance. Great achievers don't just persevere in the face of adversity; they use the pain of adversity to improve and turn their life around for a life-time. Are you in a state of giving up on your decision because you have tried everything you can but the problems keep mounting pressure and putting you through unexpected adversities? My advice to you is to keep at it with deeper commitment and use every lesson you are learning from it to flip the coin around for your greatness. You are almost there. Don't give up on yourself.

⯇ To See Ourselves Beyond Our Limitation

Stepping up and facing life's challenges courageously will equip us with the ability to see ourselves beyond the confines of our limitations. We become more confident and move faster than we ever thought was possible. Acting courageously is the only enigmatic power that will enable an individual to defy the law of limitation and push through significant hardship whenever he feels he has reached the end of his ability. To become more successful and overcome physical or mental limitations we must refuse to be defined by our worries, anxieties and the fear of impossibilities. We must imbed courage in our daily routine by doing more of what we are scared of.

Aside from immunizing us from the entrapment of fear that can make us a prisoner of self-limitation, unstoppable courage will bring out the best in us and open us to the possibility of creating success beyond our wildest dreams. The name Nicholas James, also known as Nick Vujicic, might ring a bell to those who are addicted to inspiration and personal development like me. Nick was one of the great inspirational speakers of our time. He was an Australian born without arms and legs but he did not allow this to limit or prevent him from creating a life that is barely recognizable. Nick is an incredible man who faces life with courage, despite his inability to walk, care for himself or even embrace those that he loves heartily. Throughout his childhood, Nick dealt with the typical challenges of schooling and adolescence, questioning the purpose of his life and constantly wondering why he was different from all the other kids in his class. At the age of eight, he contemplated suicide and even tried to drown himself in his bathtub at the age of ten but his love for his parents prevented him from following through. The key turning point into Nick's life came when his mother showed him a newspaper article about a man dealing with a severe disability. This made Nick realize that he wasn't unique in his struggle so he began to courageously embrace his lack of limbs, knowing within himself that he could help others change their perception about their disabilities. Nick became an inspirational speaker at 19 and since then he has managed to touch the lives of over one billion people with his story of overcoming his physical and mental limitations.

Too often we allow our circumstances to define the boundaries of our ability. Nick's story should be a wakeup call that will encourage us to act courageously toward our heart's desire because we have not limitation except for the ones we create for ourselves. Let courage be your rode and staff as you journey toward your breakthrough. As Dale Carnegie famously said, *"Most of us have far more courage than we ever dream possible."*

Cultivating Your Desire for Courage

Discipline and training of our mind is key to the development of courage. Although we won't normally schedule circumstances in which we may need to show forth our manly courage, we must prepare ourselves and be ready for any situation that requires our art of bravery. Even if we are not working or living in situations that require us to train for unexpected circumstances, we still have to prep our mind positively for daily challenges. Being courageous in any situation will allow us to trust our ability to stay focused on the achievement of our set target and realize that we are bigger than any challenge that will corner us during the process of creating the reality of our dreams. Courage is a habit that we must exercise at all times. As Marianne Williamson once said, *"It takes courage to endure the sharp pains of self-discovery rather than choose to take the dull pain of unconsciousness that would last the rest of our lives."* Here are some of the ways that we can harness our courage.

1. Go Outside of our Comfort Zone

Breaking the chain of fear and self-limitation that keeps us in our comfort zone is essential for courage mastery. There is no room for adventure and excitement in our comfort zone. In truth, the comfort zone is not really about comfort. It is an avenue for breeding fear, procrastination, weaknesses and self-limitation. By limiting ourselves to doing certain things in certain ways and resisting any form of change we are missing out on great opportunities that life is willing offer. The comfort zone is the greatest enemy of progress that keep our mind only on easy tasks by showing us only weakness and not our strengths in other areas of life. We all have both and that is where our uniqueness lies. Admitting that we have both strengths and weaknesses and are willing to create some unique things out of our potential, irrespective of what we already know, is the number one strategy that will enable us to courageously step out of our comfort zone. If you find you become too comfortable in one area of your life the solution is to explore other avenues that are open to you and become more confident that something good will come out of it that will lead you to your next level in life. Don't be your own enemy of progress by remaining in your comfort zone. Be bold and courageous to step out of it. It is not too late to be the best version of you.

2. Do Things that Others Don't

Boosting or harnessing our courage isn't a process that happens overnight. It entails daily practice and doing what others feel is impossible to achieve. To accomplish what others cannot accomplish you must be willing to place yourself in a situation where the outcome is unknown and you are determined to go the extra mile to do what others wouldn't do in that same situation. Why is this experience so important to our life purpose and accomplishment? Growth requires that we take courageous actions and launch ourselves into unknown situations for character building and mental toughness. Aside from that, constant self-challenging keeps us humble and opens us to new ways of living that may be better than what we already know. Doing what others wouldn't do isn't just about the fun of the experience; it is also about shaping our life's philosophy and challenging our beliefs.

One of the major reasons many people fail to do things that others wouldn't like to do is because of the fear of being different from everyone else. The key fact about life is that when we stop worrying about what others think and set out to achieve our heart's desire we will help others confront their own lack of belief in themselves and we will also do something that is beyond our own imagination.

3. Get to the Heart of our Fear

Fear has a way of dissociating people from their integral selves if they haven't got the confidence to defend themselves from its negative outcome. We all have fears but getting to know our fears gives us the strength and ability to overcome them. To gain a deeper understanding of what we are afraid of we must courageously look our fear in the eye. When we make a decision to expose ourselves to what we are afraid of our fear begins to shrink. As Ralph Waldo Emerson once said, *"Do the things you fear and the death of fear is certain."* Fear will always be present in our life but our ability to use it courageously to create opportunities that will lead us to the achievement of our goals is the key to greater success. To get unstuck from our fear we must confront it by acting on what we thought we were incapable of doing in spite of the risk and the danger that we might experience during this encounter. If we discipline ourselves enough to endure the pain of getting into the heart of our fear, fear loses its control over us and we will increase our level of success and happiness. Always remember that your major responsibility in life is to have the courage necessary to face every situation honestly and do whatever it takes to become successful in what you desire. Don't play the games of cowardice with your future.

"Success is not final, failure is not fatal: it is the courage to continue that counts."

-Winston Churchill

QUICK REFLECTION

1. Our ability to see beyond our limits lies in our bravery. What does being courageous mean to you? Can you give an example?

2. Looking at your previous achievements and how you have conquered what seems impossible to you, what courageous actions are you most proud of?

3. What are some of the reasons why mastering the act of courage is highly essential to success actualization

4. In what situation in life did you fail to act courageously and how can courage be applied to help you get to where you want to be?

CHAPTER 10

THE GIVING IS THE
LIFELINE FOR LIVING

"Happiness doesn't result from what we get, but from what we give."

-*Ben Carson*

The science of giving is an illogical approach that teaches us to look beyond ourselves. Giving is an art and its spirit defies the law of emotional reservation. People who want to make a positive impact on the planet fill their soul with generosity and present their time, money and expertise to the world. The truth about giving is that one is the contributor and not the receiver. As Winston Churchill once said, *"We make a living by what we get but we make a life by what we give."* Serving others through our generosity holds the key to a lot more in life than we can foresee, beyond the simple goodness of the heart. Giving has a greater power to change lives. It can give us the energy and the life blood to survive situations and circumstances that we think we cannot possibly endure. Giving in whatever form helps us get out of our head. When we help others, we are also benefiting ourselves by becoming a positive force in the universe, enhancing a community hope with opportunities and making a stranger's day.

Having the will to care for others is one of the best and the easiest ways that we can connect with our true identity. Our happiness is tied to our giving and our giving is linked to our living. As Edwin Louis Cole succinctly puts it, *"The degree of loving is measured by the degree of giving."* Dr. Anant Bhati is an angel with a cheerful heart who gave is life to save others. As a gynecologist and obstetrician, he devoted 40 years of his life to shepherding the birth of a new life into the world and donating himself to the living of others. Dr. Anant's generosity and cheerful giving made him beloved by his patients and strangers, who tells stories about how he helped them at their time of profound difficulty and need. He was an organ and tissue donor whose selfless wish was to give everything he had including himself as a sacrifice to save the lives of others. In February 2012, Dr. Anant passed away after suffering a traumatic brain injury. Even in death this generous disciple of hope didn't stop helping people. If I may beg of you to stop a little at this point and reflect on this intriguing story of wonderful giving, as you ponder Dr. Anant's story ask yourself the cheapest question that is worth more than what any currency of the world can ever buy. <u>What will the world look like if we are willing to give our life for others without expecting anything in return</u>? Let the answer to this question live with you any time you see someone in need of your help.

When we give to the less fortunate, we are not only adding to their lives we are also reinventing ours. As Bryant McGill asserted, *"Giving is the master key to success, in all applications of human life."* The art of giving kindly cultivates self-worth and opens us to unending life opportunities. Evidence from various scientific studies on giving found out that generous donors and philanthropists who give tens of thousands of their money and belongings to good cause experience greater happiness throughout their life time. The more we are willing to give, the more fulfilled we will become. Get addicted to giving.

Giving is a Gift

The philosophy of giving is an act of righteousness that comes from our duty on the earth as human beings to help each other. Zig Ziglar said it beautifully: *"You can have everything in life you want if you will just help enough other people get what they want."* Help others kindle happiness and growth. People who specialize in helping others have increasing life satisfaction and a more positive wellbeing. The intriguing story of the sixty-nine-year-old Texas resident illustrate how the power behind giving of ourselves as a sacrifice for the life of a stranger can turn around the future of generations. Brenda Jones, who was dying as her liver was failing, spent almost a year hoping and waiting to receive a call from the hospital for a perfectly matched organ for her liver transplant. She knew that she would live only if someone else's life ended. When Brenda's time to receive the liver; transplant came she was faced with a seemingly impossible decision while waiting for surgery. Her doctor made an unusual request, asking if Brenda would give her spot to a stranger who happened to be a 23-year-old newlywed woman that was airlifted to the hospital because she had suffered complete liver failure and had hours to live if she didn't get a new liver.

Brenda made an incredibly selfless decision and gave her long-awaited organ replacement spot to save the life of Abigail Flores, who was desperately in need of the organ. Brenda was put back on the waiting list for a new liver and she got her second chance at life four days later when she received a new organ transplant of her own. Brenda's kindness and compassion shows the ability to feel a stranger's pain and give everything you have to help them work through the pain. This uncommon act of kindness revealed we can create a meaningful life through purposeful giving. Whenever you find a stranger that is in dear need of your help always remember that you have the ability to feel another person's dream by helping them to open doors that might otherwise have remained closed. In fact, Mollie Mati asserted, *"Helping others in need is not only a responsibility of life; it is what gives meaning to life."*

Helping others will not only increase our happiness and life satisfaction if we engross ourselves in it, it will also open doors to great opportunities that will change our future forever. Carol Ryff, a psychologist, found one overarching idea from the writings of numerous philosophers and thinkers of history: helping others is the central feature of a positive, well-lived life. If you want to live a satisfactory life and be remembered for all your good deeds, if you want to accomplish great things and make a significant impact on the lives of others, then you have to be a cheerful giver. Now that we know what giving and compassion can bring to our life, it is time to dive deep into why it is important to give without holding back.

The Significance of Giving

For centuries, great thinkers and philosophers have suggested that it is better to give than to receive, because happiness is found in helping others. Their statement supports the anecdotal evidence that giving is a powerful pathway to personal growth and a fulfilled life. Fulfillment in life is often found in becoming a part of something bigger. Giving to a cause that can change other people's lives drastically is an extraordinary way of letting people know that their life matters to us as a community. Here are some examples of the usefulness of being "otherish" which Adam Grant, the author of Give and Take, defines as being willing to give more than you received.

❖ **Giving Boosts Your Self-Esteem**

A great deal of research evidence in psychology has shown that giving is good for our health and emotional well-being. Jennifer Crocker and Amy Canevello, University of Michigan psychologists affirm this with their statement. *"Nothing makes you more happy and proud of yourself than knowing that you are making a positive difference in the lives of other people."* Giving to others can improve how we see ourselves and the value of our contribution to the lives of others. People who give to others or donate their time and resources have been found to have higher self-esteem and overall wellbeing.

When we assist people in need, the part of our brain responsible for the feelings of happiness and fulfillment becomes active and enables us to build a positive relationship with ourselves, which increases our self-esteem. Giving can force us to get out of our comfort zone and bring out the best version of ourselves. When our actions are focused toward giving for the betterment of others, we are more likely to step up and do more than we think we are capable of. Giving cheerfully to others has a profound effect on our brain chemistry, which promotes joy and realigns us with our sense of purpose. The more we give the more confidence we have in ourselves. Showing compassion and giving not only improves our self-worth, it can also uplift us when we are experiencing a rough time. We grow by giving. Experts confirmed that performing acts of kindness will elevate our mood and make us more positive and optimistic.

❖ Giving Improves our Relationships with Others

John Holmes once said, "*There is no exercise better for the heart than reaching down and lifting people up.*" Being able to give to those in need will help us achieve a greater sense of personal satisfaction and fuel strong symbiotic relationships. The gift of giving always comes in full circle; that is why generosity is contagious. Seeing the world through someone else's eyes will undoubtedly give us the wonderful ability to be a more compassionate person. As Albert Schweitzer wisely commented, "*The purpose of human life is to serve, and to show compassion and the will to help others.*" People are naturally attracted to a person who have an open heart to share with others without obligation or expectation of it being returned.

Giving is essential when it comes to building a lasting relationship with others. When we give generously from our heart we are putting other people's needs before ours. The benefit of this is that it builds a strong connection that strengthens the relationship with the person that we give to and our act of kindness can have a domino effective that can lead to the enrichment of other people's lives. If we help someone there is tendency that they are more likely to do the same for someone else. Lending a helping hand is one of the easiest way to connect strongly with other people and make a difference in their life. We can improve the global village with one act of kindness at a time.

❖ **Giving Does Make a Difference**

Making a positive difference in the lives of others through giving is one of the most amazing and rewarding experiences that one could ever have! As Kathy Calvin profoundly said *"Giving is not just about making a donation, it's about making a difference."* Giving is an ability that we all have. When we give to a cause that is bigger than our own desire we are creating a change in the world. According to World Giving Index report for 2017, 50 percent of people helped a stranger and it made a difference in their life and lives of people around them. Generous givers give because they want to make an impact in the world but the amazing delight that they feel in their heart when they offer their compassionate kindness brings a smile to their lips and spring to their steps.

The key to making a difference is connecting with people in need and offering our service, be it our time, money, advice or life experience, to support them during their trying time. Giving back brings about change that can help us to improve the life of someone and when it's genuine and truly from our heart, it will be appreciated. Why not make a difference today by empowering others to make a difference? No duty is more urgent than giving back.

The Great Question

Everyone has the ability to help in one way or another. Sometimes the simple act of being there for someone in need can be empowering. There are no greater gifts than those that come from our heart but the major question that baffles the mind of some many about being generous is how do I start giving or what can I give to make a difference and impact the lives of others in need? The good news is, there are lot of ways we can become a generous giver to good causes and discover the transformative power of helping others. Here are some simple ways to give back to the world.

- **Volunteering** – One of the best ways to truly give back is by volunteering. When we volunteer, we may see real changes that our effort contributes and the effect of those changes on society. Volunteering offers vital help to people in need and it has a positive effect on the community. Through volunteering we can challenge ourselves to try something different, which can lead us to the possibility of learning new skills and gaining experience that can advance our career. Volunteering is a great way to connect and communicate with others and people of like minds. People volunteer for many reasons. It may be to support the cause that we are passionate about or to make a difference. Volunteering is an eye-opener to the realization that doing something small can have a huge impact in the lives of others because it means a lot to them. According to scientific research evidence volunteering can also help the volunteers to counteract the effects of stress, anger and anxiety.

Aside from providing the volunteers with a natural sense of accomplishment, pride and identity, volunteering can help volunteers develop a solid support system and keep them mentally stimulated. Doing voluntary work provides you with renewed creativity, motivation and vision that can enhance your ability to build a successful personal and professional lifestyle. Most volunteers feel fantastic and have great fun during this program, regardless of why they do it. Volunteering can be a wonderful way of changing the world if we indulge ourselves in it.

+ **Donation** – Myles Munroe once said *"The value of life is not in its duration, but in its donation."* Donation is a gift given either physically or financially form. It is a pathway to life transformation and community development that creates consistent change. Offering a donation to others is a gesture that is filled with social solidarity and great happiness. It makes you realize that even if you don't have much, you have enough to share with someone. We give donations for the purpose of providing relief and pleasure for the people in need. Donations can change the lives of people in need and drastically improve their standard of living. It can bring hope to the hopeless and help them see that others care.

When we donate to the world's neediest people we are not only changing their lives, we are also changing ours. The amazing thing about charitable donation aside from being a blessing to the receiver is that it can also bring more meaning to the life of the giver. Having the knowledge that we are actually using the little that we have to help others change their situation can be hugely empowering and makes us feel good about ourselves. The power in charitable giving can strengthen our personal values and reinvigorate our lives if we experience setbacks in any area. Generous giving can be a confidence builder and a natural repellant of self-hatred. Donating our time, money or resources is a wonderful experience that will turn our life around for good if we can give ourselves to it. Be part of the giving trend.

- **Organize Talent Shows and Fund Raising Events** – According to a recent survey of Millennials, 80 percent of people believe it's essential for people to come together in person to promote positive change, and this can be achieved through charitable event organizing. Funding raising, talent shows and miles marathon runs are another unique way of encouraging people to become generous and compassionate givers. These events provide people with a great way to get involved in their communities and offer their skills, money and other resources for societal needs.

These benevolent compassionate giving strategies can boost community spirit and give people the opportunity to make a difference in their own small ways. According research findings, one in five people attend an event to support a particular cause that is close to their heart and to show their generosity. An event of this kind teaches us to appreciate what we have and creates a greater sense of self-esteem, which can lead to better life choices. Charitable shows and event organizing are very honourable ways of providing opportunities and help for people less fortunate than we are. You can also be part of this achievement-driven giving by looking for opportunities based on your own areas of interest and skill set.

The Beacon of Hope

Sir Nicholas George Winton has passed away but his name will forever live in people's hearts. When this humanitarian prophet, born in West Hampstead, was 29 years old he received a phone call from his best friend asking him to forego his holiday plans which he had already pre-arranged for skiing in Switzerland and come down to Prague because his help was urgently needed. When Winton arrived in Prague, he was asked to help in camps filled with thousands of Jewish families, refugees living in pitiful and appalling conditions. Winton found out that the children of the refugees and political opponents from Sudetenland who were Hitler's enemies weren't being looked after. He was convinced that Jewish families and political opponents would be at risk from the Nazis when the German occupation of the rest of the country followed. His belief was strengthened further by the violence against the Jewish community in Germany and Austria during the Kristallnacht riots. Winton became determined to at least help the children of some of the families. He tried to get permits to Britain for the children but the conditions which were laid down for bringing in a child by the British bureaucracy, which was complacent and slow in their response due to their belief that there was no urgency as war was deemed unlikely, was a warranty of £50 deposited for their eventual return to their own country and a family that was willing and able to look after the child.

The situation was heartbreaking for Winton because the deposit was quite a large sum of money in those days, considering the number of children that he had in mind and many of the refugees hadn't the price of a meal. Irrespective of the obstacles and everybody telling him there was no organization in Prague to deal with the refugee children and that nobody would let the children go on their own, Winton was ready to start a mass evacuation. He independently set up his own children's rescue operation section on the dining room table at his hotel in Wenceslas Square in Prague, initially using the name of the British Committee for Refugees from Czechoslovakia, without authorization and began taking applications from anxious parents, who gradually came to understand the danger they and their children were in. His office distributed questionnaires and registered the children.

Because he had a lion heart for giving and wanted to save the lives of as many of the endangered children as possible, Winton raised money to fund the transportation of the children and find British families willing to care for them. This Holocaust hero worked at his regular job on the stock exchange by day and then devoted his late afternoons and evenings to planning the transportation of the children to Great Britain. As a result of Winton's compassion and generous devotion to be a cheerful giver and a gift of hope to other, 669 children came to Great Britain on transports that he organized. To his surprise, it was arranged for him to meetup with 669 people that owe their lives to him on BBC's **"That's Life"** program. What could be as good as being a lifesaver through your giving and generosity? Giving is a clarion call that we all must respond to if we want to become phenomenal. *Are you ready to be a giver and not a getter?*

"We rise by lifting others." -Robert Ingersoll

QUICK REFLECTION

1. Giving is a powerful weapon when it comes to a life of fulfillment. In your view, having digested the message in this chapter, what does it mean to give cheerfully?

2. Giving is an element of our true identity; without it we are incomplete. List three reasons why you think cheerful giving is significant to the achievement of our vision.

3. Do you consider yourself a generous giver? When was the last time you give whole heartedly? Discuss three simple ways to give back to the world without expecting anything in return.

4. Name one charitable cause that you will commit yourself to totally from today.

   Remember, a promise is an act of commitment to sincerity.

CHAPTER 11

GET INSPIRED BY FAILURE

"The absence of failure is the enemy of correction. Let the mastery of failure empower you with the ability to design success."

-Ayo Jimmy

The key uniqueness about the word failure is that, it is no respecter of anybody and it does not discriminate. Failure is the thin line between acceptance and fear, and when we are afraid to fail we don't engross ourselves in any risky activity, that will guarantee our success. Screwing things up isn't a diversion from our life journey to great achievement; it is part and parcel of it. Great successes are built on the foundations of failures because failure is inevitable. It teaches us things that nothing else on earth could have taught us. Failure without lessons learned is stagnation and leads one to giving up. To succeed in anything in life we are bound to fail over and over again but it is not the failures that determine our possibility for success. It is the lessons that we learn at the hands of failures that create unstoppable success. As J.K Rowling, wisely observed, *"It is impossible to live without failing at something, unless you live so cautiously that you might as well not have lived at all – in which case, you fail by default."* Any society that shuns failure and stops making failure acceptable has the tendency to discourage innovation. If we don't fail in the process of creating something that has never been created before, we are moving far away from originality.

According to evidence from various studies, eight out of ten people fail the first time they do something and seventy-five percent of all billionaires have been bankrupt at least once in their life. To drive the point home, ninety-five percent of businesses fail within the first five years. Failure is not an alien to our world; it is part of who we are and our ability to take it as part of life eliminate the imprisonment of the fear of failure. As Mickey Rooney once said, *"You always pass failure on your way to success."* When we embrace our failure, it shows that we are imperfect and that empowers us with the ability to try again. Failure propels imagination, which leads to consistent creativity. In failing we learn why the things we have ignored were actually important to the achievement of our success. People who haven't experienced failure have fewer occasions on which they can look deeply into themselves and understand what makes their motivation unshakable. Albert Einstein was considered a failure from an early age because of his inability to speak until he was nearly four years old even at that, his speaking wasn't fluent until he became twelve. His teacher had written him off with her opinion that Einstein would not amount to anything but through perseverance and willingness to fail he repeatedly learnt his way to success.

In fact, the failure he encountered was what made it possible for him to achieve what he did and become the genius that we know about today. Zig Ziglar once asserted, *"Failure is an event, not a person."* Our level of failure does not determine who we become but it can encourage us to look at situations and circumstances from a different perspective. Failure will kindle achievement if we embrace it and constantly improve our performance through the lessons that we learn from it. As Truman Capote once said, *"Failure is the condiment that gives success its flavour."* Highly successful people see failure as an experiment for growth, and that empowers them to pick themselves back up after they have been knocked down. They know that the bigger their failure, the greater their chances of succeeding. Always remember that the quickest road to success is to possess a positive attitude toward failure. A successful embrace of failure will enhance a radical change in the way we look at situations and life events when we experience them.

Greatness is Fueled by Failure

Failure is part of the fabric that makes the great achievers who they are today. Through history, there have been thousands of famous failures that have snatched success from the jaws of defeat. One of the world-known figures in this league is Harland David Sanders, 'The Kentucky Fried Chicken' found whose chicken recipe was turned down one thousand and nine times before it was finally accepted. Great achievers use failure as a tool to identify the plans that are not working so that they can continuously design a unique strategy that will work at the end. As human beings, we are not just wired to survive, we are built to strive in the face of adversity and to learn at the feet of failure. As Winston Churchill affirmed, *"Success is the ability to go from one failure to another with no loss of enthusiasm."* In order to remain motivated, committed and focused on doing what it takes to become an achiever, we have to learn to respond positively to setbacks because *"setbacks are setups for a comeback*," says Willie Jolley, the author of It Only Takes a Minute to Change Your Life. Having a positive attitude toward failing will help us feel better and make us realize that every good thing takes time.

The intriguing story of Soichiro Honda, who turned failure into fortune, is a testimony that shows that every success is ninety-nine percent failure and it takes time. Eight years after Japan was badly hit by the great depression of 1930s, Soichiro Honda started a little workshop with a burning desire to develop the concept of piston rings and sell his ideas to Toyota Company. He laboured night and day and even slept in the workshop, always believing that he could perfect his design and produce a worthy product. Because he struggled financially during this period he sold his wife's jewelry for capital. After several months of sweat and toil he completed his working model of piston ring. With high expectations Honda took his piston ring design to Toyota, who told him that the rings did not meet their standards. He came back to his workshop with a shattered dream. After suffering this terrible setback, Honda was forced to go back to school and the other engineers laughed at his design. He was broke and frustrated but he wasn't about to give up on his dream easily. Rather than focus on his failure, Honda continued working hard toward his goal. He spent the next two years finding ways to make the piston ring better without letting anyone disturb his concentration. Then, after two years of struggling and redesign, he won a contract with Toyota. With contract in hand Honda needed a factory to produce his supplies but due to the Japanese government's preparation for the Second World War building materials were costly and in short supply. Despite this potentially disastrous setback, he persisted and found a new way of making concrete which allowed him to build the factory needed for his supplies, but the factory was bombed twice during the war and steel became unavailable. While most people would have given up at this point, Honda found a way to get past life's adversities. He started collecting surplus gasoline cans discarded by US fighters, which became new raw materials for his rebuilt manufacturing process.

Sadly, this was not the end of Honda's life lesson, as the factory he had struggled so hard to rebuild the second time was leveled it to the ground by an earthquake. This setback would have spelled the end for most people but Honda's belief in his vision still made him carry on. After the war, Honda found a way of attaching a small engine onto his bicycle and quickly found that other people were interested in his new idea. He made so many of these bicycles that the entire town ran out of small engines and he was unable to meet their huge demand. Honda's dream received another deadly attack but his resilience to strive through life's obstacles kept him in line with his dream. Rather than giving up he sought out a way to get the finance he needed to continue with his project. Honda wrote letters to over 18,000 bicycle shop owners asking them to help him revitalize Japan. Five thousand bicycle shop owners responded and advanced him the little money they could to build his tiny bicycle engines. He battled away with several innovations before Super Cub, which became an overnight success, was finally produced. Honda succeeded because of his ability to embrace failure and see it as a learning curve for greatness. I don't know what failure that you have experienced in the past or the setbacks that you are facing at the moment. If you remain persistent and never allow yourself to give up, you will surely fail your way to success at the end if you don't quit. Your success is on its way!

The Real Reason Why Embracing Failure is Crucial to Success

Failure is one of the aspects of life that most people are afraid to experience. But the truth is everyone has failed at something and everyone will continue to fail at something. It is not the failure that counts but what you do after failing that determines the true reality of who you are and what you become. So, do not be afraid of failing. As Thomas Watson once said, *"If you want to increase your success rate, double your failure rate."* Rather than hiding from our mistakes or feeling sorry for ourselves for failing, if we embrace our failure and see it as a great lesson from life, we'll be in a better position to learn and succeed on our next attempt. Here are some of the real reasons why embracing failure is crucial to our success.

➢ **Failure Helps You Grow**

Failure, as much as it hurts, is an important part of life's lesson that helps us grow. Our ability to deal with obstacles when we are driven into a small corner by failure and still have the strengthen to forge ahead is a test that will sharpen and grow our character through discipline. When we fail, we reflect on the causes of our failure and that enables us to develop a new meaning from the painful situation. Every failure that we experience has an underlying lesson that accompanies it and with the right mindset, we can turn the wheel of this painful situation to our own benefit by learn from it and using the knowledge as a guide to build unimaginable success.

Using the lesson that we learning from failure to fuel success will enhance our growth because it will open us to the possibility of starting all over again with new ideas. As Henry Ford once said, *"Failure is only the opportunity to begin again, only this time more wisely."* Instead of fearing failure we must embrace it as a creative spark and use it to amplify our ability to grow in all life situations. Failure will surely happen no matter how hard we try to avoid it, so we might as well have a no-fear attitude toward it. Remember that every failure is one step on the stairway to success.

➢ Failure Builds Character and Humbles You

There is a lesson to learn from everything, including failure. Failure teaches us more about ourselves and by doing so it helps us to make regular adjustments to our character. As Billy Dee Williams brilliantly commented, *"Failure's not a bad thing. It builds character. It makes you stronger."* Somewhere inside every failure hides the teaching that models and structures our character to be humble. Failure encourages better thinking and gives us true confidence to acknowledge our mistakes so that we can learn from our disappointment. It holds us accountable for our actions by reminding us of the reason why we do what we do. Through the doctrine of failure, we learn to put our character to check and this strengthens our ability to withstand the pain of failing.

Failing at something that we thought we knew by heart makes us humble because we immediately realize that as humans we are not perfect and we are vulnerable to making mistakes. Occasional failure is a useful reminder that despite our hard work, sometimes things can go wrong it is bound to happen. Failure fosters resilience that helps us trust ourselves more when we learn from it and embracing it empowers us to overcome the odor of procrastination and inaction.

➤ Failure Spark Your Creativity

Failure is a medicine with a therapeutic function that can help our subconscious mind to bring creativity to life. The relationship that we have with failures, particularly how we see them and respond to them, has a way of encouraging us to upscale our craft and become more creative. We can become discouraged by failure or we can use it as a tool to unleash our creative side. According to Brene Brown, *"There is no creativity without failure, period."* Life is about learning the wisdom of creativity through failure and since failure is an unavoidable part of life that sparks creativity, we have to embrace it. Ironically, <u>it is our struggle with our own failure that brings the best out of who we are.</u> The experience of failing to get what we want, most especially when we have worked so hard for it, can help us to figure out a way to succeed by any legal means necessary. To bring out the best of our potential we must try out new things without the fear of failing. Failure allows us to gain a better idea of what to change or improve on. The more setbacks we experience in life the more failure pushes us to master creativity.

➤ Failure Opens us to Better Opportunities

We appreciate success more when we've tasted defeat or rejection, because greater opportunities come through defeat. You might have experienced a situation where you were turned down for a particular offer which you think was the best option for you at that point in time, only to receive another opportunity somewhere else that was far better than the previous offer. Rejection or failure does not mean that is the end of things. It only implies that you should try the same activity again but this time with more knowledge and wisdom to handle the situation. As Ira Glass noted, *"If you're not failing all the time, you're not creating a situation where you can get lucky."* Failure is not a special gift reserved for a particular set of people but a phase that every one of us must go through in order to create better and more successful opportunities. Knowing that failure is part of life's teachings that we have to experience will make us stand our ground every time we face challenges. It's easy to perceive failure as misfortune but to overcome life's tests we must embrace failing. The people who learn how to master their failure and convert it to an unimaginable opportunity are the most successful people in the world. *Let the lesson from failure make you your own master and not the slave.*

How to Embrace Failure with a Positive Attitude

Poet Samuel Beckett is known for his profound statement, *"Ever tried. Ever failed. No matter, try again. Fail again. Fail better."* Uttering this poetic word of wisdom, he knows the importance of failing and why our attitude toward failure holds the golden ticket to success mastery. The difference between those who moved on to succeed and those who did not comes down to their perception and attitude toward

158

failure. Failure has always been our traveling companion on this journey called life. As Robert Kiyosaki wisely emphasized *"Failure is part of the process of success; people who avoid failure also avoid success."* Our attitude toward failure will surely have a profound effect on our behaviour and how we can turn some major failures into incredible opportunities that will not only materialize unimaginable success but will also be a blessing to the entire world. Here are some of unique ways that we can reap the rewards and gifts of embracing failure with a positive attitude.

❖ **Learn from Everything**

The attitude we create toward a particular event will determine what we will learn from it. It is true that when we fail we ponder so that we can identify what we are doing wrong and how to correct this error in judgment. To master the act of embracing failure and using it to our own advantage we must see every event and situation as an avenue to learn and gain new knowledge about life. Failures are small moments in a lifetime of experience that introduce us to regular learning and by seeing them as a snapshot in time, we are beginning to have an open mind to learning from every situation that happens to us. Although the experience of failure can be disappointing and painful, instead of allowing it to weigh us down we should see it as one of the lessons that will help us grow. As one of the great minds once put it *"Failures are part of life. If you don't fail, you don't learn. If you don't learn you'll never change."* Failure is life's greatest teacher that equips us with the wisdom to turn adversity to advantage through learning. To become the best version of ourselves we must imbibe Tilopa's philosophy by *"having a mind that is open to everything and attached nothing,"* which in itself is the foundation for learning. Always remember that you can't get something done without failing and failing is all about mastery if you have a positive attitude toward it.

❖ Renounce Perfection

We will fail forward by learning from our setbacks and making necessary adjustments until we become successful if we do not allow our need for perfection to hold us back. Perfection is a delusion that we must abstain from if we are to guarantee our success from failure, because nobody has gotten a grip on it nobody. *"Perfection is the enemy of progress,"* Winston Churchill famously answered when he was asked about perfection. We can't stop obstacles or failures from appearing in our life but we can choose how to handle them. When we seek perfection in everything we do, we will always see failure as a taboo. No one is perfect and no one can do everything perfectly. If we accept that we are all imperfect creatures and understand that there is only so much we can change in any given situation, we will learn to embrace failure with a positive attitude. Successful people renounce perfection but embrace hard work with a positive mindset, which gives them the strength, wisdom and motivation to face obstacles with resilience and tenaciousness. If they can do it you can do it too. Don't let chasing perfection keep you in fear of embracing failure with a positive attitude.

❖ Turn Mistakes into Motivation

When our attitude is right, we can achieve maximum results in things that others perceive as improbable. Having a positive attitude toward failure can ignite our inner desire to turn our mistakes to an opportunity that will yield massive success. We can create an attitude shift that will propel our ability to turn mistakes into motivation by reading and listening to material that shares the biographies of people that have experienced failure and how they use it to conquer self before they fulfilled their dreams. Instead of viewing our failure as humiliating and disappointing, we must learn to use it as energy to invigorate us to try again and again until we fulfill our heart's desire. As George Edward Woodberry once mentioned, *"Defeat is not the worst of failures. Not to have tried is the true failure."* We cannot avoid failure but we can learn from it by consistently trying and motivating ourselves to be open to new opportunities that will lead us to great achievement. Learning to see the value in even the most trying experiences can be the difference between giving up and persevering. All in all, we must use failure as fuel to energize us in turning our adversity to our advantage and not be used by it to create our down-fall.

❖ Keep a Positive Mind

Since our subconscious mind can only hold one thought at a time, either it chooses positive or negative. If we deliberately choose the positive thought to dwell on, that keeps our emotions positive and our mind optimistic. *"Positive thinking will let you do everything better than negative thinking will,"* says Zig Ziglar. One of the biggest secrets to embracing failure with a positive attitude is starting to look for the good in every situation that happens in our life. When we look for the good in situations, it reflects on our attitude and that empowers us to take positive steps in creating unprecedented success. Optimism correlates with resilience and strong coping techniques in times of adversity. Positive thinking not only promotes success, it also develops confidence and self-esteem that helps us recognize and find opportunities. Much of our ability to succeed comes from the way we deal with failure and optimistically manage the disappointment with the stress that comes with it. Research proves that optimism equips us with more positive ways of overcoming challenges and embracing failure with a positive attitude. Adopting positive thinking as a way of life will create an unimaginable change that will increase our happiness and pave the path for us to fail forward instead of seeing failure as a defeat. To achieve our personal best and reach unparalleled heights in making the impossible possible we must continuously develop the state of mind that is linked to positive thinking. Don't let a poor attitude toward failure be the reason you stay in a state of mediocrity forever.

"Don't fear failure. Not failure, but low aim. is the crime. In great attempts, it is glorious even to fail."

-Bruce Lee

QUICK REFLECTION

1. The lesson of life is not only encrypted in success hand writing but it also has a manuscript version for failure where the biggest experience of life grows from. In your own opinion, why do you think it is important to celebrate our failures?

2. After reading through this chapter, what are some of the lessons that you have learned about failure which you will use to motivate yourself when you experience failure on the battle-ground of life?

3. Failure is inevitable; it is our ability to master it and turn it upside-down through the creation of opportunity out of it that counts. Identify three reasons why embracing failure is vital to our success.

4. What is the great advice that you would give to the young version of you about failure?

CHAPTER 12

GRATITUDE IS THE
KEY TO HAPPINESS

"The miracle of gratitude is that it shifts your perception to such an extent that it changes the world you see."

-Dr Robert Holden

If there's one thing that affects our happiness more than anything else, it's gratitude. Gratitude is an art of thanks giving that opens doors to favour and happiness. *"Gratitude generate growth and growth leads to greatness."* says Ayo Jimmy. The word gratitude indicates a positive emotion that is felt after being the beneficiary of some sort of gift which is undeserved. When we cultivate the habit of being grateful for everything that happens in our life, it enhances our ability to turn challenging situations around for good and create unimaginable greatness. Being grateful just for being alive is a great way to motivate oneself to seize the day. A well-thought-out thank you instead of half-hearted complaining and whining, often leaves people feeling pretty good and happy. When we are grateful for little things that we get, we have the tendency to get more from the people we appreciate for giving the help or gift.

Aside from that, this heart of thankful and deeper appreciation for what we receive has a way of improving our health and wellbeing. Expressing gratitude costs nothing, yet has so many valuable benefits associated with it. As Melody Beattie profoundly expressed, *"Gratitude makes sense of our past, brings peace for today, and creates a vision for tomorrow."* Rather than giving up in defeat, rebelling in anger against life or living life as a victim, having a grateful heart has a way of changing our perception about circumstances. Although it is not an easy virtue to master when we are deeply overwhelmed by life challenges our ability to see our situation as a stage in life that we all have to go through in order to get to our next destination in life and be grateful for it will enable us to overcome.

Gratitude is a wonderful thing that is extremely valuable to practice every day of our life. In gratitude, we turn on the light that illuminate wonder and gives that peace of mind that make us believe that we have the power to change our situation. As Deepak Chopra professes, *"Gratitude opens the door to the power, the wisdom, the creativity of the universe. You open the door through gratitude."* It is easier to complain about our life until we find someone else's life to compare ours to; then we realize how grateful we should be for the things we have and the ones we have not. We all have something to be grateful for. The more grateful we are for small and simple acts that we experience in life, the more satisfied we will be in life. And that will open doors to greater opportunities. Even when life seems very challenging, showing appreciation for the wonderful gifts and blessings that are already present in our lives can help to foster a stronger sense of happiness and wellbeing.

Turning gratitude into a habit takes away anxiety, stress and

Worry. It helps us connect to something larger than ourselves as individuals. From good health to positive feelings there are incredible amounts of things that we need to be thankful for each day of our life. *"When you look at life through eyes of gratitude, the world becomes a magical and amazing place"* This brilliant statement from Jennifer Gayle shows how mightily the word gratitude holds the key to our sense of contentment and happiness. Until we learn to be grateful for the things we have the chance of receiving what we want is very slim. Find a reason to be grateful for every single day and write a thank you note to someone for how they make you feel; it will change your life for good.

The Record of Truth with the Lyrics of Gratitude

"All the members of the human society stand in need of each other's assistance, and are likewise exposed to mutual injuries. Where the necessary assistance is reciprocally afforded from love, from gratitude, from friendship and esteem, the society flourishes and is happy." This is an inspirational thought of Adam Smith expressed in words without knowing of the world that it has its mirror image reflected in the riveting true story that I read about an entangled whale's gratitude. According to the story teller, a female humpback whale was entangled in a spider web of crab traps and lines which wrapped hundreds of yards of line rope around her body, with a line tugging in her mouth. The hundreds of pounds of traps weighted her down, caused her to struggle and stopped her from staying afloat. A fisherman on daily fishing business spotted her just east of the Farallon Islands and radioed for help.

Within a few hours, the rescue team arrived with a cavalry of helpers. Assessing her situation, they came to the conclusion that she was badly injured and the only way to save her life was to dive in and untangle her, which was a very dangerous proposition. One slap of her tail could kill the rescuers. They worked for hours with curved knives and eventually set her free. When she observed that she was freed she swam in a joyous circle and then came back to each and every diver, one at a time, and nudged them and pushed gently, thanking them in her own unique way. The incredibly beautiful experience of gratitude dropped the divers' jaws for hours. If animals can understand the power that lies behind gratitude so can you. Be grateful for everything and let the power of gratitude use Mother Nature to surround you with the people that will help you get untangled from every adversity that life drops at your feet.

The Surprising Benefits of Gratitude

Being grateful for all that we have in life is one of the keys to true happiness and it doesn't cost a penny or require much of our time. Cultivating gratitude is one of the simplest routes to a positive attitude and improved mental health. Often, we tend to forget that our happiness doesn't come as a result of us getting what we want but rather by our appreciation of what we have. Counting our blessings and being grateful for them on a regular basis not only enhances our optimism, it will also lead to a satisfactory life. Here are some of the proven benefits that you will enjoy for being grateful.

❖ **Gratitude Improves Self Esteem**

The practicing of gratitude has a spillover effect; it allows us to reflect on what we have achieved, our positive life experiences and the lives of people we have touched. Gratefulness makes us feel better about our circumstances and appreciate our accomplishments and those of other people more. It can encourage us to improve on our moral behaviour and our outlook on life in general. As Oprah Winfrey expressed, *"The single greatest thing you can do to change your life today would be to start being grateful for what you have right now. And the more grateful you are, the more you get."* Having gratitude is a powerful way of making us feel better about ourselves by keeping us in the present and not allowing us to dwell on past negative experiences. Consciously expressing thanks daily can help us cope with stress and trauma. Whenever we count our blessings we make the good things of life visible and that works to help us improve our wellbeing. Gratitude can help us unleash our self-confidence and inhibit invidious comparisons with others.

❖ **Gratitude Unshackles us from Toxic Emotion**

Learning to heartily say thank you can change our life and improve our well-being if we cultivate the culture and implement principle every time we receive a gift or experience life challenges. The art of counting our blessings and being appreciative for what we have and what we have not has a way of uplifting the spirit by unshackling us from negative emotions. Gratitude research evidence has repeatedly shown that gratefulness improves our psychological health and reduces stress. When people are grateful for what they have, they generally perceive life from an enhanced perspective and that enables them to make the best use of what they already possess. As wisely affirmed by the Secret, *"Gratitude is a power process for shifting your energy and bringing more of what you want into your life."* When we are grateful for what we already have, we will attract more good things in life. Mindful gratitude helps us develop kindness and increase our mental strength. Developing the attitude of gratitude is one of the simplest ways to reduce a multitude of toxic emotions like envy, frustration and regret.

❖ **Gratitude Strengthens Relationships**

The feeling of gratefulness helps us to identify people that are responsive to our need and brings us closer to them. This emotion of gratitude not only motivates us to build a symbiotic relationship with another person but it also turns ordinary moments into an opportunity for relationship growth. Gratitude is one of the keys for promoting strong intimacy in any relationship. Research evidence on gratitude reveals that being appreciative for a gift from a stranger or new acquaintance can make them more likely to seek an ongoing relationship. Mindful appreciation for gestures offer by partners, friends, coworkers or acquaintances can greatly strengthen the bonds of friendship and help create a flourishing relationship. As Steve Maraboli once said, *"Gratitude is the nutrition for living relationships."* People who are grateful tend to express their appreciation to others and that helps them win more friends and deepen their existing relationships.

The emotion of gratitude improves satisfaction for both the recipient of appreciation and the person expressing the appreciation. Taking time to let people know how grateful we are for their generosity will not only promote a sense of connectedness but will also increase our relationship. If we regularly take the time to express gratitude in everything we do it will surely strengthen our relationships and make us happier. The practice of gratitude will boost the bonding of relationships if we master it and express it in every situation. So, it is important that you let your life be rooted in gratitude because it will transform your life and create fulfilling relationships.

❖ Gratitude Makes Us Happier

Fostering gratitude help to reorient our mental compass toward focusing on the positive by relishing our good experiences broadens our thinking and improves our state of health. Sincere gratefulness from the heart leads to a more sustainable form of happiness and it brings us closer to fulfilling our heart's desire. The practicing of gratitude tends to give us a more positive, happier outlook and a sense of perspective. As David Steindl-Rast once said, *"Happiness is not what makes us grateful, it is gratefulness that makes us happy."* Learning to be grateful will bolster your self-worth and propel immeasurable joy that will continuously lift your spirit of happiness. By taking pleasure in appreciating some of the gifts of nature and the goodies of life you will be able to extract the maximum possible satisfaction and enjoyment from your current circumstances. According to University of California Davis psychologist Dr. Robert Emmons, people who are thankful for their blessings are happier and they have an optimistic outlook toward things. A grateful state of mind will not only help us achieve greater happiness and fulfillment; it will also improve our well-being. Expression of gratitude is the cornerstone of happiness and being open to it is the only way to remain happier and have an authentic life style; don't leave it to chance.

How to Foster Gratitude into our Lives

Gratitude has the ability and the power to bring us peace and serenity if we learn to cultivate and express it. As Zig Ziglar wisely affirmed, *"Among the things you can give and still keep are your word, a smile and a grateful heart."* Counting our blessings and being grateful for them is not only for a recipe for a fulfilled life but also a ticket to greater achievement and life transformation. Whenever we are short changed in the area of gratitude, the fear of losing something or not getting what we think we want tends to set in and that bring about negative thinking and emotions. The only way to turn this around for our own good is to establish a daily gratitude resolution as a strategy to help us ensure that we never under pay our dues of gratitude. Here are some of the ways that we can incorporate gratitude into our lives.

Keep a Gratitude Journal

Sometimes we tend to forget some of the things we need to be grateful for but having a gratitude journal and listing down both the positive and negative things that have happened in our life will act as a constant reminder to shift our perception to the one of love rather than of fear. Journaling the series of events in our life will not only make us a gratitude addict, it will also enable us to express empathy toward others. A gratitude list makes us solution oriented and enables us to build resilience with the possibility of seeing ourselves already overcoming the challenge like we did with previous obstacles. Keeping a gratitude diary can reinforce our positive thoughts and help us to be more progressive as we work passionately toward our personal goals. If you want to find a smaller way to live a more grateful and fulfilled live, keeping an archive of your list of blessings by setting aside five to ten minutes daily before bed is one unique way to do this. You can take a step further by creating a gratitude ritual vision board where you can put your list of things you are grateful for in a designated area of the board. My wife uses a gratitude jar where she pops all her list of events to be grateful for and at the end of every month she opens the jar and reads through her notes while verbally casting her vote of thanks in a bigger way. Cultivate the habit of journaling your list of gratitude today; it will energize your ability to see yourself better than you are.

⚜ Model and Teach Gratitude

Be an emblem of gratitude and preach the gospel to the world by using your good and bad times to inspire people to set themselves free from complaints, worries, anxiety and fear. Expressing gratitude through words, writing and giving of small gifts or acts of reciprocity opens doors to opportunity and increases not only your happiness but the happiness of other people around you. *"Our favorite attitude should be gratitude,"* as Zig Ziglar wisely affirmed. When you practice the heart of gratitude by showing it through your way of living and praising the people that have been kind to you, it boosts their self-esteem and brings them to a state of joy that is beyond their imagination. Being thankful is a valued attitude that gives us a heightened sense of appreciation for the things that are happening in our life. Illustrating gratitude daily through our action isn't just a nice thing to do; it's good for our health because it helps us to reduce toxic emotions that create depression, envy and regret. While we may not know, what lies ahead of us each day, starting our days with a grateful, positive state of mind will make any difficult moments that come up a bit easier to handle. Gratitude is a social emotion; finding a way to share it with the people around you will not only reinforce your positive feeling, it will also empower others to do more good in the world.

⚜ Volunteer your Time

No matter how old we are, nothing fills the voids in our lives like building a great relationship with people we love and the people around us. Spending time with the people we love and giving our time to good causes is one of the most powerful ways of imbibing the culture of gratitude. DeAnn Hollis expressed the importance of this statement through her profound words: *"The heart of a volunteer is never measured in size, but by the depth of commitment to make a difference in the lives of others."* Giving helps foster gratefulness and blessing others with our time is a huge part of that. When we model gratitude through generous volunteering what we learn from such experiences is far greater than what we give. People who make time to help others usually feel grateful for the experience because it allows them to use their talents and skills in a meaningful way. Expressing gratitude by giving of our time to help others achieve their innate desires is a humbling experience that increases our social bonds and grows our circle of influence. When we give, we grow and that empowers us to bring out the best version of ourselves. Carving out time for our loved ones and people around us shows that we care and are grateful to have them in our life. A life well-lived is the one that is full of gratitude. Help others fulfill their dream by giving them part of the peace of your precious time.

⬥ Live in the Moment

Developing a gratitude mindset and habit requires more than attitude; it involves living in the moment with great appreciation for whatever you have and the things around you. Acknowledging the moment and being grateful for everything within creates freedom and unimaginable happiness. Living for the moment is about taking notice of the smallest of all things and being grateful for them. Our normal healthy state of being alive is a wonderful gift and should be treated as one. Always remember that your present situation is not your final destination; it is the best you have for the moment so enjoy it and be grateful for it. Spending time focusing on what may happen next down the line tends to rob us of fully experiencing what is happening right now. It is very essential that we live and love each moment as it comes because before we know it the precious time will slip away from our sight. To perform our best in life we must react positively to the moment with a joyful heart and believe that every day comes with its own opportunities and challenges. We show love to ourselves and show kindness to others. Above all, we must live with the belief that the good and the bad things of life happen to teach us lessons that will help us to create the best version of ourselves. Become addicted to intentional gratitude.

"May you experience all the levels of thankfulness and soul-gifts that each offers, for then it will be truly possible to give and receive joy every day of your life."

-MJ Ryan

QUICK REFLECTION

1. Gratitude is the ultimate perspective shifter that paints our life with a positive focused brush. Why do you think it is very important to make gratitude part of the ongoing fabric of our lives?

2. Gratitude gives us true clarity and focus on how our successes can come to be. List three ways to foster the act of gratitude in our lives.

3. Identify four things in your life that you are taking for granted and you know you need to be grateful for.

4. List three privileges that you can benefit from for being grateful.

EPILOGUE

DON'T THINK, DON'T TRY- JUST DO IT

I congratulate you for finishing this book. It is my sincere hope that you have acquired the knowledge that you will need to help you kick-start the process of your life transformation and continuous life time achievement. However, the most important thing to remember is that it is not what you learn that counts but the actions that you take to implement what you learn and how quickly that you take those actions that matter. Consider this: *"Learning is power but acting massively is the superpower."* Resolve today to become intensely action oriented by practicing every concept you have mastered in the last twelve chapters of this book. It will revolutionize your life and revamp your thinking and your possibilities. The world is waiting for you to step up into your greatness by living up to your true potential and bringing out the best version of you!

-AYO JIMMY

CLOSING WORDS

Writing this book was an incredible undertaking that took a year and seven months of research, writing and rewriting. This book has emerged from thousands of hours of interviews given by great and highly successful people in every area of life, business and sports. Through the process of writing this book my life has been one long continuous process of personal and professional development, including reading lots of books and research papers and attending innumerable seminars and workshops.

One thing that became so clear me throughout this journey is that whatever we desire or aspire for in life is possible if we are ready to pay the price of belief, positive mindedness and work hard. We are all blessed with a talent that can enhance our ability to create the best version of ourselves but the key to exploring this talent is knowing that we have something special that we need to give to the world. I don't know who you are but one thing I know for sure about you is that you are more powerful than you can ever imagine and you can leave your mark on the golden walls of this planet if you don't quit chasing your dreams. Don't give up on yourself!

Thank You Notes

First and foremost, I want to thank God Almighty, the father of all wisdom and inspiration.

My special thank you also goes to a group of special people who believed in me and my vision to let me interview them and shared their life experiences for this amazing book. I am overjoyed to get to tell your journeys. Your time, generosity and achievement-driven support is invaluably appreciated.

The finishing of this book is a true testament to the spirit of collaboration. I would like to say a big thank you to my wonderful sister, Mrs. Nwando Okoh. She was the one who carefully and tirelessly read every version, made every edit and helped develop every idea, no matter how late at night I sent her a piece of work. Thank you to Miss Mulenga Nkamba for proofreading the whole book and offering innovative suggestions on how use the contents of this book to engage readers. As my first reader, she helped shape this book and saved the rest of you from several boring stories. I would also like to thank my mentor Michelle Watson for her support and good advice. I hope you know what an inspiration you've been to me all my life.

To Olaoluwapo and Ifeoluwapo, you two are treasures for putting up with me during the process of writing this book and waking up at night to proofread parts of my work. You are the light in my heart that fuels my passion for greatness!

Thank you to Eddie and Sue Edwards for encouraging me to follow my heart. I'd like to thank my sister and family for their prayers and motivation. Your love and support is what molded me into what I am today. I owe you everything for that.

Most of all, I am grateful to the Adenusi family for their inspiration and support in finding my purpose. My vote of thanks goes to Dr. Tala and Mr. and Mrs. Akioya for their wonderful support and Jolly you are a true friend.

To everyone who reads and believes in this book, I wish you every success.

Scan the code to see other collections from Ayo Jimmy on Amazon

Don't miss out on other collections from Ayo Jimmy

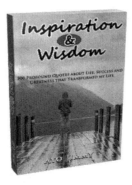

Inspiration and Wisdom:

"This book is an excellent toolkit for dealing with adversity and life challenges." Swindon Advertiser

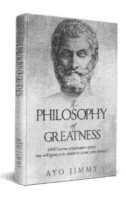

The Philosophy of Greatness:

"Teaches you how to find inner happiness and your purpose for living." It is a classic inspirational work.

The Power of Words

"What Ayo Jimmy does so masterfully in this book is to provide you with insight on how to increase your hunger to strive for more by dispelling the myths about fear, faithlessness and doubt that have overshadowed your ability to use your potential to amass your unlimited greatness." One of the most powerful self-improvement books.

BOOKS THE AUTHOR RECOMMENDS

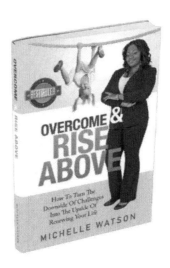

Overcome & Rise Above

With the growing number of children diagnosed with ADHD, this brings attention to the many challenges faced by parents who have ADHD-diagnosed children and other behavioural or learning disabilities. The author provides usable tips on how to overcome the difficulties of ADHD, and points the way for creating a successful future for your child. She offers appropriate coping strategies and excellent tools for improving life, not just for your child, but for your entire family. The journey always begins with parents, so author Michelle Watson reveals the challenges faced by many mothers including abuse, depression and fear. *Overcome And Rise Above* advises readers on how to break out of the cycle of failure and doubt, and will set you and your family on a pathway of success.

Rise Above & Believe

With the growing number of people that are giving up on their dreams, allowing excuses and their circumstances to hold them back, this book brings attention to the many challenges that individuals face on their journey of creating the life they desire. Michelle Watson in this book provides examples, stories, facts and experiences on how to rise above those hurdles and create your desired life.

Printed in Poland
by Amazon Fulfillment
Poland Sp. z o.o., Wrocław